D1583069

# L S W R
## LOCOMOTIVES

Urie 'H15' class No. 476 and Maunsell 'King Arthur' No. 785 *Sir Mador de la Porte* at Waterloo on 26th September 1936.

*J. H. L. Adams*

AN ILLUSTRATED HISTORY OF

# L S W R
# LOCOMOTIVES

THE

## URIE CLASSES

*including those modified and built by*

**R. E. L. MAUNSELL**

BY

## D. L. BRADLEY

# WILD SWAN PUBLICATIONS LTD.

© Wild Swan Publications Ltd. and D. L. Bradley 1987
ISBN 0 906867 55 X

## ERRATA TO PREVIOUS VOLUMES

The coupled wheel diameter quoted for the 'O2' class 0—4—4Ts on page 60 of *The Adams Classes* should read 4 ft 10 ins not 4 ft 0 in as shown.

The drawing on page 213 of *The Drummond Classes* depicts a C8 Class express engine, not a T9 as marked on the original drawing and thus incorrectly titled.

Designed by Paul Karau
Typesetting by Berkshire Publishing Services
Printed and bound by Butler & Tanner, Frome

Published by
WILD SWAN PUBLICATIONS LTD.
1-3 Hagbourne Road, Didcot, Oxon OX11 8DP

# CONTENTS

# INTRODUCTION

London & South Western locomotives have a special appeal to railway historians for most were designed and built by well-known and highly respected mechanical engineers since Joseph Beattie, William Adams, Dugald Drummond and Robert Urie all completed distinguished careers in charge of the company's locomotive department. With some 1,500 engines involved, the history cannot be contained by a single volume, therefore this part of the survey only covers the Urie classes.

In pursuit of knowledge, the engine, boiler and tender registers, drawings, diagram books, coal returns and the rough notes of the Locomotive Committee meetings made available by the staff at Eastleigh Works in 1965-6 proved invaluable. Reference was also made to the minute, account and other registers held by the Public Record Office at Kew and to the Nine Elms and Eastleigh drawing office registers, drawings and photographs in care of the National Railway Museum at York. In all instances the dates of ordering, construction, entry to service, modification, rebuilding, reboilering, withdrawal, breaking up and sale have been taken from the engine and boiler registers, which detail all the engines owned by the South Western from 1841 to 1922, details of which are confirmed and amplified by the Nine Elms and Eastleigh Works repair journals of 1892-1932. For the later period, use has been made of the Southern Railway and British Railways engine, tender, boiler and frame cards, the Waterloo mileage registers, the weekly works return sheets and notices of withdrawal, breaking up and sale. Assistance was also sought from the Sharps Stewart, Dübs, Neilson, Robert Stephenson and Beyer Peacock order books and

drawings preserved by the Science Museum, South Kensington, the Greater Manchester Museum of Science & Industry and the Mitchell Library, Glasgow.

The dimensions were obtained from the South Western and Southern Railway diagram books, general arrangement drawings and the order books of private manufacturers. Unfortunately, these sources often fail to agree, while it was not unknown for Nine Elms and Eastleigh to issue contradictory figures. The company's weights in working order were computed for engines in light steam with 5 cwt of coal in the firebox, 2½ in. of water showing in the glass, full tender, saddle or side tanks and 5 cwt of coal in the tender or bunker. As a result, these weights, particularly the tenders, were considerably less than those appearing in the manufacturers' order books, Board of Trade accident reports, weigh house records and Southern Railway diagram books. Dimensions and weights, like final mileages, are not an exact science.

Engine allocations before Grouping have often caused historians difficulty, but fortunately many of the lists issued each year in March by Nine Elms Works recording the current position of the engine stock, including those away for repair, have been preserved. After this establishment closed, responsibility for these lists was transferred to Waterloo, where those for 1878-1922 were available in 1965. Human nature being what it is, all railways are beset by accidents, although by good fortune and able management, the South Western only suffered one major disaster, at Salisbury in June 1906. All accidents, trivial or serious, have to be reported and the subsequent Board of Trade or Ministry of Transport accounts of the events leading to

1

Urie 'S15' class No. 499 and Drummond 'L12' class No. 426 at Eastleigh in 1923.

R. C. Riley Collection

the incidents provide useful sources of train formations and speed, company practice, dimensions, weights, mechanical details and repair mileages.

Nine Elms ex-works dates almost invariably indicated the date when construction or repair was completed, with a further two or three weeks elapsing for painting and trial running before revenue earning service was entered. At Eastleigh Works, the date of transfer from yard to the nearby running shed was recorded as the entry or return to traffic, despite most engines requiring further attention by fitters sent across from the works. After Nationalisation the entry to traffic dates recorded by the engine cards were entirely fictitious, for their main purpose was to ensure on paper that the specified quotas of general, intermediate and casual repairs were being completed. Often the entry to traffic was a month or more after the official date.

This book could not have been written without the help of many people too numerous to name individually. However, special thanks are due to Peter Swift, chairman of the South Western Circle, Ted Fry, photographer supreme of Salisbury, Sid Nash, John Edgington and the late George Woodward, who recorded all the Eastleigh Works arrivals and departures from mid-1926 to the end of steam.

# ROBERT URIE
## MECHANICAL ENGINEER 1912-1922

DUGALD DRUMMOND died in office on 8th November 1912 and the following month was succeeded by Robert Urie, his friend and works manager since 1897, first at Nine Elms and later Eastleigh. Previously Urie had been associated with Drummond on the Caledonian Railway, a lengthy partnership which enabled him to appreciate the good and indifferent features of his chief's locomotive practice. He was also fully aware of the South Western's need for successful six-coupled passenger engines, therefore after cancelling a proposed Drummond class of doubtful prospects, he fulfilled this requirement with his 'H15' class.

After World War I these capable mixed traffic 4–6–0s were followed by basically similar classes for express passenger and heavy main line goods service, while powerful 4–6–2 and 4–8–0 tanks for London area interchange goods and hump shunting completed his 'Big Engine' policy.

Urie was an early exponent of superheating and following successful trials with the 'H15' class, he applied this feature to all his own engines as well as to many designed and built by his predecessor. At first the products of Robinson and Schmidt were employed, but by late 1914 he had designed and patented the Eastleigh superheater.

All his classes were robustly constructed, accessible and without frills, whereas the Drummond 4–6–0s were complicated with most of the features demanding regular maintenance artistically concealed. There were only two large cylinders and these with the Walschaerts valve gear were outside the frames and fully exposed by the high running plate. The coupled wheel bearings measured 9 ins by 12 ins, while the plain split brass big-ends with straps, cotters and bolts, replaced Drummond's marine-type. Similar principles were extended to the boiler, where conventional fireboxes, injectors and barrel clackboxes

replaced firebox cross water tubes, Duplex feed pumps and front tubeplate clackboxes. If Drummond's 4–6–0s were works of art, then Urie's were strictly functional.

The rejection of needless complexity also applied to the tenders, where the outside bearings, springs and frames were separate from the water tank and supported by two carriage type bogies, a construction which gave a massively strong vehicle capable of working high mileages between repairs and unlikely to suffer the leakages of the Drummond 'water carts'.

After Grouping the three 4–6–0 classes, with some modification and improvement, were perpetuated by Maunsell for service on the Southern Railway.

National Railway Museum

'N15' class No. 748 in Urie livery when new.

# LOCOMOTIVE LIVERIES

## URIE LIVERIES

### Passenger Classes

After taking office Urie retained the Drummond livery, without the splasher coat-of-arms and with some lining variation on the 'H15' class, until December 1914 when the royal green was replaced by olive green. Urie referred to the colour as sage green, but this it certainly was not for it was marginally softer and darker than the Drummond green and akin to a ripe green olive.

The dark brown bordering and intricate lining remained until October 1917, when wartime economy caused a change to a 3 in. black border separated from the olive green by a fine white line. The boiler bands were black with white edging and the outside cylinders olive green with a black band edged by white at the extremities. Drummond style numerals and lettering remained in use.

After some months weathering and cleaning, the olive green became more yellow, which probably accounts for the confusing references to the hue in contemporary railway journals.

### Goods Classes

Holly green with black edging and white lining was in use until late 1917, when the lining was often omitted to save labour and materials until after the Armistice.

## R. E. L. MAUNSELL

### Passenger Classes

All the early Eastleigh Grouping repaints were in Urie livery, but from November 1923 the white line separating the black border from the olive green was changed to yellow and 'Southern' inscribed in 6½ in. extended primrose yellow lettering across the tender or tank sides above similarly coloured 18 in. numerals. Until mid-1931 a 3 in. letter 'E', also in primrose yellow, appeared between the lettering and numerals on Western Section engines to distinguish them from those of the Eastern (A) and Central (B) Sections. After the first eleven Southern repaints, small oval brass numberplates were attached to the cab sides and tender backplates of tender engines and to the bunker backplates of tank engines. At first the background was black, but from mid-1928 this became buffer beam red. On the front buffer beam the E-prefix appeared on the left of the draw hook and the numerals in 5 in. characters to the right.

In February 1925 the Urie olive green was superseded by a deeper and more attractive green, known as Maunsell green, while the line edging the black bordering reverted to white. When the E-prefix was removed, 'Nº' appeared to the left of the front draw hook, the numerals remaining to the right.* At the same time the tender and bunker backplate numberplates were removed and replaced by transfer numerals below the coping.

* From about 1929 until the renumbering of 1931 the prefix 'E' appeared to the left of the draw hook.

### Goods Classes

The Urie holly green livery remained in use until November 1923, when it was replaced by black with dark green lining. The style followed that of the passenger classes and the same changes occurred.

### 'S15' Class

The original livery was goods black, but because of their regular use on passenger trains, this was changed to Maunsell green from February 1928.

### Goods Livery Lining

To save expense this was omitted after mid-1935, the first Drummond engine to enter traffic plain black being '700' class No. 691 in August 1935.

### Side Tank Numerals

Commencing with Nos. 46 and 246 in August 1931, the 'M7s', 'C14s' and 'K14s' were given 15 in. instead of 18 in. side tank numerals.

## O. V. BULLEID

### 'King Arthur', 'N15' and 'H15' Classes

The first indication of a livery change came in May 1938 when 'N15' class No. 749 was painted brilliant unlined light green by Eastleigh Works. Block numerals replaced the small cabside numberplates, while one side of the tender was conventionally lettered 'Southern' and the other 'SR' in very large block capitals. It would appear that the colour was considered too bright for the following month No. 749 was painted a less startling green (later known as malachite) with black and white lining and 'Southern' applied to the tender in lined block lettering. On one side the numerals were painted on the cab sides and on the other the smoke deflectors. No. 749 was returned to traffic in Maunsell livery, but the second experimental style with cab side numerals formed the basis of the new Bulleid liveries. These came in three shades of green, Maunsell, olive and malachite, with black/white, black/yellow or green/yellow lining. Full details will be found with the respective classes. Because of World War II plain black became standard in March 1942. After the cessation of hostilities, the 'King Arthurs' and 'N15s' were painted malachite green, but the 'H15s' remained black.

### Secondary Passenger Classes

The Maunsell green livery, with minor lining variation, remained in use until September 1939, when repaints were either unlined Maunsell or malachite green with cab or bunker numerals and Bulleid lettering. The use of green ceased because of wartime shortages in March 1941, when plain black became standard. After the war the royal 'T9', No. 119, and a handful of 'M7s' were painted malachite green, but otherwise plain black remained in use until after Nationalisation.

5

'H15' No. 331 with E-prefix in Maunsell livery.
*Author's Collection*

**Goods Classes**

These remained plain black with Maunsell lettering and tender or tank numerals until September 1939, when cab or bunker numerals and Bulleid lettering became standard.

## BRITISH RAILWAYS

The 'King Arthurs' and 'N15s' continued to be painted malachite green until August 1949, when Brunswick green with orange and black lining was substituted. Secondary passenger classes, including the 'H15s', were painted black with red, cream and grey lining and goods classes plain black. Numerals appeared on the cab or bunker sides and number plates were attached to the smokebox doors. Full details of these liveries and the temporary S-prefix are contained in the text.

### LIVERY REFERENCE DATES

| | |
|---|---|
| British Railways lettered tender and tank sides | January 1948 |
| Smokebox numberplates | June 1948 |
| Unlettered tender and tank sides | December 1948 |
| 1st British Railways totem | August 1949 |
| 2nd British Railways totem | March 1957 |

### POWER AND LOAD CLASSIFICATIONS

| Classes | Urie | 1st BR | 2nd BR |
|---|---|---|---|
| 'N15' | A | 5P | 5P |
| 'King Arthur' | A | 5P | 5P |
| 'H15' (both series) | A | 4MT | 4P5F |
| 'S15' (both series) | A | 6F | 6F |
| 'G16' | A | 7F | 8F |
| 'H16' | A | 5F | 6F |

## ENGINE DISC AND LAMP BRACKETS

When Urie took office in December 1912, disc and lamp headcodes were displayed on six brackets, at the top and on either side of the smokebox, and three on the platform above the buffer beam. Apart from the transfer of the two smokebox side brackets to the door in the 1930s (in the case of Urie and Maunsell locomotives often coincidental with the fitting of smoke deflectors), these positions remained standard until the end of steam, although the arrangement of headcodes changed at intervals over the years.

BR number and power classification on 'H15' class at Eastleigh on 26th March 1955.          *E. W. Fry*

'N15' No. 737 *King Uther* in malachite green livery with Bulleid lettering, at Oxford in 1948.          *G. Coltas*

'H15' No. 30332 in BR mixed traffic black livery with red, cream and grey lining and first British Railways small totem on the tender, at Guildford on 19th April 1952.          *Author*

## ENGINE HEADCODES 1911-1917

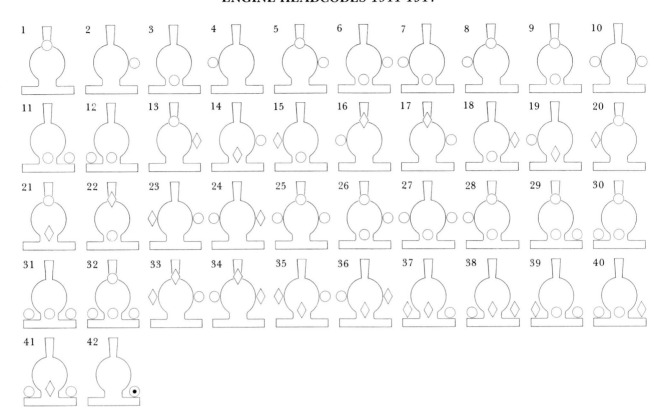

1. Kensington & Woking via Richmond. Guildford & Farnham. Waterloo & Wimbledon Pk. Sidings, via East Putney (Empty Trains). Eastleigh & Bulford via Chandlersford & Andover. Southampton Docks & Brockenhurst & Dorchester via Wimborne.* Weymouth & Portland & Easton (Passenger Trains). Plymouth & St. Budeaux.
2. Waterloo or Nine Elms & Southampton Docks via Main Line. Willesden & Brentford via Gunnersbury.
3. Waterloo & Kingston via Kensington. Staines & Weybridge. Brockwood & Bisley Camp. Alton & Fareham. Bentley & Bordon. Fort Brockhurst & Lee-on-the-Solent. Hamworthy Jn. & Hamworthy. Salisbury & Bulford. Axminster & Lyme Regis. Tipton St. John & Exmouth. Plymouth & Cattewater. Winchester (Cheesehill) & Southampton Docks.** Barnstaple (GWR) & Barnstaple Jn. & Ilfracombe.** Bodmin (GWR) & Wadebridge.** (Great Western Co's Trains, see Notes).
4. Waterloo or Nine Elms & Reading, via Loop Line. Willesden & Brentford via Kew East Jn. Weybridge & Virginia Water. Guildford & Aldershot. Exeter & Sidmouth.
5. Waterloo or Nine Elms & Guildford, via Leatherhead. Waterloo & Wimbledon via Main Line. Waterloo or Nine Elms & Southampton Docks via Brentford, Chertsey & Woking. Salisbury & Dorchester via Wimborne.*
6. Waterloo & Kingston & Shepperton, via East Putney. Ludgate Hill & Richmond New, via Kensington. Brentford & Neasden via Kew East Jn. Woking & Windsor, via Byfleet Curve, Southampton Docks & Andover. Basingstoke & Alton.
7. Waterloo to Waterloo via Twickenham, Whitton Jn., & Hounslow. Brentford & Brent via Kew East Jn. Wimbledon Station or Durnsford Rd. Sidings & Waterloo, via the Main Line (Empty Trains).
8. Waterloo or Nine Elms & Hampton Court. Waterloo & Twickenham via Barnes. Waterloo & Shepperton via Twickenham. Brentford & Brent via Chiswick Jn.
9. Waterloo or Nine Elms & Plymouth. Clapham Jn. & Twickenham via Kensington & Chiswick Jn. Battersea & Brent, via New Kew Jn. Southampton Docks & Portsmouth via Netley. Windsor & Ascot via Staines High Street.
10. Waterloo or Nine Elms & Guildford via Cobham. Waterloo or Nine Elms & Reading via Twickenham. Clapham Jn. & Kensington. Ascot & Farnham. Guildford & Godalming Goods. Eastleigh & Portsmouth. Salisbury & Bournemouth West via Wimborne.
11. Waterloo or Nine Elms & Woking via Richmond & Chertsey.
12. Waterloo & Nine Elms Goods Yard.
13. Waterloo or Nine Elms & Windsor via Twickenham. Woking & Chertsey & Reading, via Virginia Water Curve.
14. Waterloo & Wimbledon Pk. Sidings via East Putney (Passenger Trains). Southampton Docks & Nine Elms, via Main Line (Market Goods, Fruit, or Potato Trains).
15. Southampton Docks & Nine Elms via Chertsey & Brentford (Market Goods, Fruit & Potato Trains).
16. Waterloo or Nine Elms & Southampton Dks. via Alton. Waterloo or Nine Elms & Windsor, via Loop Line. Waterloo & Barnes & Feltham via Loop Line.
17. All stations to Nine Elms Loco Depot. Nine Elms Loco Depot & Nine Elms Goods Yard, via Engine Line or Queens Road. Portsmouth to Fratton Loco Depot. Exeter & Exmouth Jn.

18. Exeter & Nine Elms (Market Goods & Fish Trains). Southampton Docks & Bournemouth West via Sway.
19. Waterloo & Virginia Water via Main Line. Gunnersbury & Twickenham. Salisbury & Southampton West & Portsmouth via Netley. Bournemouth Central & Dorchester.*
20. Nine Elms & Neasden via New Kew Jn. All Stations to Eastleigh Loco Depot.
21. Waterloo & Clapham Jn. (Empty Trains). Nine Elms Loco Yard to Clapham Jn. Ludgate Hill & Wimbledon, via Merton Abbey. Brentford & Southampton Docks via Ascot & Farnborough Curve. Ringwood & Bournemouth West, via Christchurch. Wareham & Swanage. Exeter & Torrington.*
22. Waterloo & Waterloo Roundabout Service via Kingston. Ascot & Woking via Frimley. Southampton Docks & Salisbury via Redbridge. Exeter & Padstow.*
23. Waterloo or Nine Elms & Portsmouth, via Woking & Guildford. Waterloo & Wimbledon, via East Putney. Southampton Docks & Salisbury via Eastleigh. Fareham & Gosport. Bodmin & Wadebridge.
24. Waterloo or Nine Elms & Southampton Docks via East Putney. Petersfield & Midhurst. Havant & Cosham. Fratton & East Southsea. Botley & Bishops Waltham. Fareham & Stokes Bay. Brockenhurst & Lymington Pier. Bournemouth West & Dorchester.* Whitchurch & Fullerton. Yeovil Jn. & Yeovil Town. Chard Jn. & Chard Town.* Seaton Jn. & Seaton. Exeter & Exmouth. Barnstaple Jn. & Ilfracombe. Halwill Jn. & Bude. Plymouth Friary & Turnchapel.
25. Waterloo or Nine Elms & Brockenhurst & Bournemouth West, via Sway.
26. Kensington & Wimbledon via East Putney.
27. Waterloo & Waterloo, via Hounslow & Twickenham. Clapham Jn. & Richmond New via Kensington. Ludgate Hill & Wimbledon, via Haydons Road.
28. Waterloo & Richmond New via Kensington.
29. Nine Elms & Brent, via New Kew Jn. Weymouth & Portland & Easton (Goods Trains).
30. Nine Elms & Willesden, via New Kew Jn.
31. Shepperton & Twickenham & Willesden via Gunnersbury, Nine Elms to Nine Elms, via Chertsey & Brentford, or vice versa. Cattewater Jn. & Plymstock.**
32. Royal Trains.
33. Members & 1st Class Race Trains, via Earlsfield.
34. Members & 1st Class Race Trains, via East Putney or via Twickenham.
35. Fast Race Trains (1st, 2nd & 3rd Classes) via Earlsfield.
36. Fast Race Trains (1st, 2nd & 3rd Classes) via East Putney, or via Twickenham.
37. Stopping Race Trains (1st, 2nd & 3rd Classes) via Earlsfield.
38. Stopping Race Trains (1st, 2nd & 3rd Classes) via East Putney or via Twickenham.
39. Waterloo & Hampton Court, via East Putney (Excursion Trains).
40. Waterloo & Leatherhead & Guildford via East Putney (Excursion Trains).
41. Waterloo & Oxshott & Guildford, via East Putney (Excursion Trains).
42. Special Train:- By Day: White Disc with Black Centre. By Night: Purple Light.

NOTE

\*   Trains running over the GWR will carry the GW Co's Code.

\*\* GW Co's Engines will carry unlighted lamps instead of disc shaped boards by day.

## ENGINE HEADCODES 1921

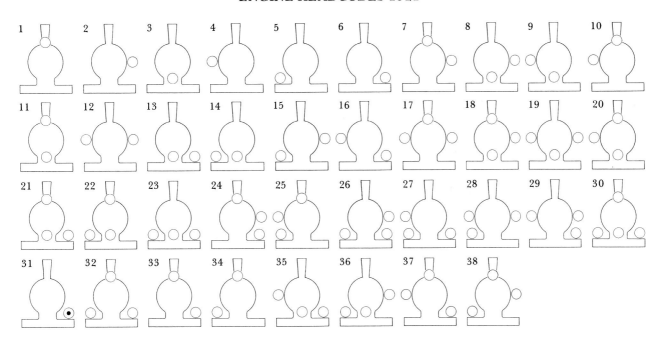

1. Waterloo & Wimbledon Park Sidings via E. Putney (Empty Trains & Light Engines). Brentford & Twickenham via Whitton Jn. Guildford & Farnham. Plymouth & St. Budeaux. Eastleigh & Bulford via Chandlersford & Andover. Southampton Docks & Brockenhurst & Dorchester via Wimborne. Weymouth, Portland & Easton (Passenger Trains). Woking & Chertsey & Reading via Virginia Water Curve. Exeter & Torrington. Bodmin & Wadebridge. Petersfield & Midhurst. Botley & Bishops Waltham.
2. Waterloo or Nine Elms & Southampton Docks via Main Line. Willesden & Brentford via Gunnersbury. Waterloo or Nine Elms & Windsor via Twickenham. Southampton West to Lymington (Through Trains). Fareham & Stokes Bay. Havant & Cosham. Yeovil Jn. & Town. Whitchurch & Fullerton. Chard Jn. & Town. Seaton Jn. & Seaton. Exeter & Exmouth. Barnstaple Jn. & Ilfracombe. Halwill Jn. & Bude.
3. Staines & Weybridge. Brookwood & Bisley C. Alton & Fareham. Bentley & Bordon. Salisbury & Bulford. Axminster & Lyme Regis. Fort Brockhurst & Lee on Solent. Hamworthy Jn. & Hamworthy. Tipton St. Johns & Exmouth. Plymouth & Cattewater. Winchester (Cheesehill) & Southampton Docks. Barnstaple (GWR) & Barnstaple Jn. & Ilfracombe. Bodmin (GWR) & Wadebridge. Ludgate Hill & Wimbledon via Merton Abbey. Ringwood & Bournemouth West via Christchurch. Wareham & Swanage. Ascot & Woking via Frimley. Brockenhurst & Lymington Pier.
4. Waterloo or Nine Elms & Reading via Loop Line. Willesden & Brentford via Kew East Jn. Weybridge & Virginia Water. Guildford & Aldershot. Exeter & Sidmouth. Plymouth Friary & Turnchapel. Waterloo or Nine Elms & Hampton Court.
5. All Stations to Nine Elms Loco.
6. All Stations to Eastleigh Loco.
7. Waterloo or Nine Elms & Guildford via Leatherhead. Waterloo & Wimbledon via Main Line. Waterloo or Nine Elms & Southampton Docks via Brentford, Chertsey & Woking. Salisbury & Dorchester via Wimborne.
8. Brentford & Neasden via Kew East Jn. Exeter & Exmouth Jn. Southampton Docks & Andover via Redbridge. Nine Elms Loco Depot to Nine Elms Goods Yard via Engine Line or Queens Road. Portsmouth to Fratton Loco Depot. Bournemouth West to Dorchester. Kensington to Woking via Richmond.
9. Waterloo or Nine Elms & Richmond via Kensington. Brentford & Brent via Kew East Jn. Exeter & Padstow. Salisbury & Southampton West & Portsmouth via Netley. Woking & Windsor via Byfleet Curve. Wimbledon Stn. or Durnsford Rd. Sidings & Waterloo via Main Line (Empty Trains or Light Engines).
10. Waterloo & Twickenham via Barnes. Waterloo & Shepperton via Twickenham. Brentford & Brent via Chiswick Jn. Waterloo or Nine Elms & Southampton Docks via Alton. Salisbury & Bournemouth West via Wimborne. Ballast Trains to Meldon Quarry from Exeter Queen St. & Fareham & Gosport (Stations West thereof).
11. Waterloo or Nine Elms & Plymouth. Battersea & Brent via New Kew Jn. Southampton Docks & Portsmouth via Netley. Windsor & Ascot via Staines Curve. Bournemouth Central & Dorchester.

12. Waterloo or Nine Elms & Guildford via Cobham. Waterloo or Nine Elms & Reading via Twickenham. Clapham Jn. & Kensington. Guildford & Godalming Goods. Ascot & Farnham. Eastleigh & Portsmouth. Southampton Docks & Salisbury via Redbridge.
13. Waterloo or Nine Elms & Woking via Richmond & Chertsey. Eastleigh Loco to Bevois Park Sidings.
14. Waterloo or Nine Elms & Southampton Docks via East Putney.
15. Waterloo & Clapham Jn. (Empty Trains & Light Engines). Nine Elms Loco Yard to Clapham Jn. Southampton Docks & Andover via Eastleigh.
16. Light Engines from Waterloo Station to 'B' Box Loco Sidings. Engines Running Round Bournemouth West Triangle to Turn. Light Engines & Empty Trains to Clapham Jn. from Stations Westward.
17. Waterloo or Nine Elms & Brockenhurst & Bournemouth West via Sway. Waterloo or Nine Elms & Windsor via Loop Line.
18. Waterloo or Nine Elms & Shepperton via Kingston. Kensington & Wimbledon via Clapham Jn. Southampton Docks & Brent via Richmond & Gunnersbury.
19. Waterloo & Waterloo via Kingston. Clapham Jn. & Richmond New via Kensington. Ludgate Hill & Wimbledon via Haydons Road.
20. Southampton & Willesden via Richmond & Gunnersbury. Parcels Trains, Waterloo & Clapham Jn.
21. Nine Elms & Brent via New Kew Jn. Weymouth & Portland & Easton (Goods Trains). Exeter & Nine Elms (Market Goods & Fish Trains). Eastleigh Loco to Southampton Docks.
22. Nine Elms & Willesden via New Kew Jn. Southampton Docks & Nine Elms via Main Line (Market Goods, Fruit or Potato Trains).
23. Kingston & Twickenham & Willesden via Gunnersbury. Nine Elms to Nine Elms via Chertsey & Brentford or vice versa. Cattewater Jn. & Plymstock. Southampton Docks & Salisbury via Eastleigh.
24. Southampton Docks & Nine Elms via Chertsey & Brentford (Market Goods Fruit & Potato).
25. Brentford & Southampton Docks via Ascot & Farnborough Curve. Waterloo & Virginia Water via Main Line. Nine Elms & Neasden via New Kew Jn.
26. Waterloo & Nine Elms Goods Yard. Woking & Kensington via Brentford & Chiswick Jn. Southampton Docks & Bournemouth West via Sway.
27. Waterloo or Nine Elms & Portsmouth via Woking & Guildford.
28. All Stations to Feltham Marshalling Yard.
29. All Stations to Strawberry Hill (Loco Depot).
30. Royal Trains.
31. Special Train. By Day: White Disc with Black Centre. By Night: Purple Light.

Nos. 32 to 38 to be carried by Specials for Race Meetings and Special Events, Advised by Special Notice.

'H15' class No. 482 in Eastleigh works yard.

Author's Collection

# THE URIE CLASSES
## 'H15' Class

During the 19th century most railways assigned 0—6—0s or obsolescent passenger engines for mixed traffic duties, but some companies, including the South Western, provided specially designed engines. This practice, commenced by Nine Elms as early as 1854 with Joseph Beattie's 'Hercules' class 5 ft. 6 in. 2—4—0s, must have proved beneficial for Adams built no less than ninety 'Jubilee' 0—4—2s to work these duties, while a similar number of small-wheeled 4—4—0s of classes 'K10', 'L11' and 'S11' were supplied after the turn of the century by Drummond. However, by 1911 four-coupled engines were no longer capable of working the more arduous duties, so Drummond designed and obtained authority for the construction of ten 'K15' class 6 ft. 4—6—0s at an estimated cost of £3,700 each. Entries for the class first appear in the Eastleigh Works Drawing Office Register in August 1912 and continue until Drummond's death three months later. Unfortunately, all the drawings listed, except those of the cylinders, appear to have been destroyed, but from notes and sketches in Drummond's work book, the dimensions were probably as follows:

| | |
|---|---|
| Cylinders (4) | 16½" x 26" |
| Bogie wheels | 3' 7" |
| Coupled wheels | 6' 0" |
| Wheelbase | 6' 6" + 6' 9" + 7' 0" + 7' 0" = 27' 3" |

| | |
|---|---|
| Boiler | 'F13' class |
| Estimated weight in working order: | |
| Engine | 74T 10C |
| Tender | 60T 10C |
| Total | 135T 0C |

Drawings of an 0—8—0, the 'H15' class, were prepared concurrently, but both designs were discarded by Urie, which was probably as well for there was little likelihood of either proving capable of overcoming the triple handicap of saturated steam, long shallow grates and tortuous front-ends.

Once in charge, Urie lost little time designing his own 4—6—0 mixed traffic class, with entries appearing in the Drawing Office Register as early as March 1913, while on 24th April 1913 authorisation was granted for the construction of ten under orders H15 and K15. Photographs of the lead engine were presented to the Locomotive Committee on 24th January 1914, while all ten, Nos. 482-91, were in service by August 1914. At this period Eastleigh was not fully committed to superheating, so two were left saturated to compare performance and fuel consumption. The costs of construction and dimensions were as follows:

Nos. 482-5 Schmidt superheater (royalties £180 each) £3,885 each

'H15' class No. 482 again in Eastleigh works yard showing the Drummond livery carried when built.          *Author's Collection*

11

'H15' class No. 487, when new, in Eastleigh works yard, carrying Waterloo or Nine Elms to Southampton Docks via Alton headcode.

'H15' class No. 482 at Waterloo in 1914.
*R. C. Riley Collection*

Nos. 486-9  Robinson superheater (royalties £200
                              each)                    £3,960 each
Nos. 490-1  Saturated                                  £3,810 each

| | |
|---|---|
| Cylinders (outside) | 21" x 28" |
| Valve gear | Lap 1", valve travel 5 1/8", lead 1/4" |
| Bogie wheels | 3' 7" |
| Coupled wheels | 6' 0" |
| Wheelbase | 7' 6" + 5' 4½" + 6' 3" + 7' 6" = 26' 7½" |
| Boiler diameter | 5' 6" |
| Boiler length | 13' 9" (Tubeplates 14' 2") |
| Firebox length | 9' 0" |

Heating surfaces:

| | Nos. 482-5 | Nos. 486-9 | Nos. 490/1 |
|---|---|---|---|
| | *sq. ft.* | *sq. ft.* | *sq. ft.* |
| Small tubes (169 x 2") | 1,252 | 1,252 | 2,025* |
| Large tubes (27 x 5¼") | 507 | 464 | — |
| Firebox | 167 | 167 | 167 |
| Total evaporative | 1,926 | 1,883 | 2,192 |
| Superheater | 360 | 333 | |
| Total | 2,286 | 2,216 | |

* 272 x 2"

| | | |
|---|---|---|
| Grate area | 30 sq. ft. | |
| Working pressure | 180 lb. | |
| Weights in working order: | Nos. 482-9 | Nos. 490/1 |
| Bogie | 20T 16C | 20T 10C |
| Leading coupled wheels | 20T 2C | 19T 6C |
| Centre coupled wheels | 20T 4C | 19T 16C |
| Trailing coupled wheels | 20T 3C | 19T 10C |
| Engine total | 81T 5C | 79T 2C |
| Tender | 57T 14C | 57T 14C |
| Engine & Tender | 138T 19C | 136T 16C |

The boiler was parallel and constructed in two rings with a round-topped firebox and an unusually large diameter smokebox, the last mentioned being accentuated by the small door and was quite different to the smokeboxes fitted to the later Urie classes. Lock-up safety valves in neat casing were sited on the firebox, while the Drummond pattern chimney was of small diameter and short, as was the dome cover which consequently became known as 'the pimple'. The cab contours followed those of the Drummond 'D15s' and 4—6—0s.

The double bogie tender was equipped with exhaust steam feedwater heating and was much more substantially constructed than those provided by Drummond. Consequently leakage was practically unknown and much higher mileages were worked between heavy repairs. The South Western diagram book records the capacity as 5,200 gallons of water and 5 tons of coal, with a fully laden weight of 57 tons 10 cwt, but after Grouping this was adjusted to 57 tons 14 cwt.

After being run in on local passenger and goods duties by Eastleigh, Nos. 482-7/90/1 were sent to Nine Elms and Nos. 488/9 to Salisbury, but by March 1915 all were working from Nine Elms. Unlike most top link passenger engines, they were double manned and extensively employed working Bournemouth and Salisbury expresses by day and heavy goods or vans at night. Some of the duties are contained in the Locomotive Committee report of August 1914, details being:

**Nine Elms  No. 482**
10.15 a.m.  Waterloo-Bournemouth Central
3.44 p.m.  Bournemouth West-Waterloo
11.00 p.m.  Nine Elms Yard-Salisbury (goods)
3.00 a.m.  Salisbury-Nine Elms Yard (goods)

**No. 483**
8.50 a.m.  Waterloo-Salisbury
12.35 p.m.  Salisbury-Exeter
4.17 p.m.  Exeter-Salisbury
8.25 p.m.  Salisbury-Waterloo

'H15' class No. 488 at Clapham Junction in 1914.
*Gerry Beale Collection*

**No. 485**
8.55 a.m. Waterloo-Bournemouth Central
3.05 p.m. Bournemouth West-Waterloo
10.45 p.m. Nine Elms Yard-Salisbury (goods)
6.50 a.m. Salisbury-Woking (fish vans)

**No. 486**
8.15 p.m. Waterloo-Salisbury
1.10 a.m. Salisbury-Nine Elms Yard (market goods)
11.20 a.m. Waterloo-Salisbury
4.12 p.m. Salisbury-Waterloo

**Salisbury  No. 489**
7.34 a.m. Salisbury-Waterloo
2.00 p.m. Waterloo-Bournemouth West
6.57 p.m. Bournemouth West-Waterloo
3.05 a.m. Waterloo-Salisbury (milk empties)

This report was guaranteed to please the most avaricious member of the Locomotive Committee, but unfortunately a later one concerning hot boxes was less encouraging, details being:

| Class | No. in Class | No. of Hot Boxes 1914-7 |
|---|---|---|
| H15 | 11 | 13 |
| T14 | 10 | 6 |
| G14 | 5 | 2 |
| P14 | 5 | 1 |
| L12 | 20 | 2 |
| T9 | 66 | 3 |
| E10 | 5 | 0 |
| T7 | 1 | 1 |
| D15 | 10 | 1 |

Urie blamed the 'H15' failing on over-rigid frame staying and the intensive working; the rigidity would be rectified at the first heavy repair. For some reason rebuild No. 335 was not so prone to hot boxes, only one being recorded in 1915-24.

As previously mentioned, Nos. 482-5 were built with Schmidt superheaters and Nos. 486-9 with the Robinson

pattern, while for test purposes Nos. 490/1 employed saturated steam. Therefore it is surprising that no actual performance and fuel consumption trials appear to have been conducted between engines of the three types. Possibly this was because of the outbreak of war in August 1914. However, a Locomotive Committee report of September 1915 gives the following mileage and coal consumption details:

| No. | Mileage Worked | | | Coal Burnt per Mile | Total Cost of Superheater Maintenance |
|---|---|---|---|---|---|
| | Passenger | Goods | Total | | |
| 482 | 29,651 | 15,967 | 45,618 | 47.4 lb | |
| 483 | 29,417 | 11,089 | 40,506 | 46.9 lb | Schmidt £121-17-11 |
| 484 | 27,982 | 10,149 | 38,132 | 49.1 lb | Robinson £108-14-2 |
| 485 | 23,005 | 10,916 | 33,921 | 50.3 lb | |
| 486 | 34,595 | 16,063 | 50,658 | 49.8 lb | |
| 487 | 30,963 | 17,472 | 48,435 | 48.7 lb | |
| 488 | 34,334 | 6,262 | 40,596 | 47.3 lb | |
| 489 | 20,861 | 11,986 | 32,847 | 47.6 lb | |
| 490 | 19,805 | 14,094 | 33,899 | 58.7 lb | |
| 491 | 20,457 | 13,171 | 33,628 | 59.4 lb | |

**Schmidt Superheater**
This system has proved to have several unsatisfactory features, the most serious being the damper which permits the gases to condense as sulphuric acid in the flue tubes and causes deep pitting of the elements. Leakage also occurs after 5,000 to 6,000 miles at the copper jointing between the element flange blocks and the header. To date no satisfactory remedy has been found to overcome these serious and time-consuming problems. *Maintenance:* The element accessibility is very poor, a faulty top row element can only be reached for attention by removing two other elements.

**Robinson Superheater (Nos. 486-9)**
Constant trouble is caused by temperature variations in the headers as the result of the saturated and superheated chambers being adjacent. Difficulties have also arisen with the attachment of the headers to the elements, although this has been recently overcome by replacing the bolting by expanding the elements. *Maintenance:* To a lesser degree the same difficulty applies as with the Schmidt pattern.

Two views showing 'H15' class Nos. 488 and 486, when new, in Eastleigh works yard. The lower view clearly shows the cab fittings following the layout established by Drummond.
*Author's Collection*

'H15' class No. 483 at East-leight fitted with Schmidt superheater.
*Author's Collection*

### Saturated (Nos. 490/1)

Both are good, strong engines with better acceleration than the remainder of the class, but are heavy on coal and water.

Because of these superheater failings, Urie designed his own type, which became known as the Eastleigh pattern and was first applied to 'H15' No. 335 in December 1914. Proving successful, it was fitted subsequently to classes 'N15', 'S15', 'G16' and 'H16' as well as to many Drummond classes and the post-Grouping 'H15s'. Its advantage lay in the ease with which individual sections could be removed, for the top and bottom headers were basically distribution chambers attached to the lower connecting pieces and alternately coupled to the upper saturated and lower super-heated headers. The four-fold element tubes commenced at the saturated header and returned to the superheater header, while the individual tubes passed through the connecting members to be secured by bolts at the front and rear, leaving the three vertically arranged elements entirely independent. In regular service complete satisfaction was given, but it was heavier and more expensive to construct than the Maunsell pattern, by which it was superseded after Grouping. Nos. 490/1 were fitted with Eastleigh super-heaters in December 1919 and October 1917, when the latter also received a short stove-pipe chimney.

As the war on the Western Front intensified and goods traffic passing over the South Western increased, so it became necessary to restrict the class to troop specials, ambulance trains, heavy goods and vans. It was while so employed on the early evening of 2nd March 1917 that No. 490 startled intending passengers standing on Winchester station by suddenly appearing out of the darkness at the head of a goods with the smokebox door slowly opening and closing to give those having the courage to stand fast the ghastly sight of an incandescent pile of ash topped by several grinning rows of tubes. Very wisely the crew, having

overcome their initial shock, had forsaken the footplate and were clinging to the cab sides. Eventually, the train, which was virtually running away, was brought under control and halted north of Eastleigh, where the door was secured. At the subsequent company's inquiry, the young fireman insisted that he had securely fastened the door before leaving Nine Elms shed and indeed it had remained firmly shut until approaching Winchester Junction, when it suddenly swung open, turning the footplate into an inferno of flames and red hot coals. After considering all the evidence, Urie concluded that the door had not been correctly fastened and blamed the crew for the occurrence, but because of their heroic attempts to stop the train, only administered a reprimand. However, this was not the last of the incident for on 24th April 1917 as No. 490, with a different crew, came to a stop at Waterloo, the door slowly swung open to the amazement and consternation of the ticket collectors and passengers standing at the barrier. Again on inspection at Nine Elms, there appeared to be nothing wrong with the door fastenings, but while the crew and the shed foremen were discussing the incident, the door obligingly sprang open. As a result, a new door was fitted and the original crew suitably rewarded.

As previously mentioned when describing the Drummond 4—6—0s, 'E14' class No. 335 was laid aside for heavy repairs at the time of this engineer's death and therefore was awaiting attention at Eastleigh Works when Urie took office in December 1912. At once he issued instructions for rebuilding as an 'H15' class 4—6—0 with two outside cylinders, Walschaerts valve gear, new main frames, improved lubrication, a conventional firebox and a 24 element Eastleigh superheater, its first use by Urie. Therefore when returned to traffic at a cost of £4,395 on 5th December 1914, No. 335 was virtually a new engine, for little more than the boiler shell, bogie wheels and tender remained of the Drummond 4—6—0. The dimensions were:

'H15' class No. 335 rebuilt from Drummond 'E14' class in 1914 and retaining the 'water-cart' tender.  *Author's Collection*

'H15' class No. 491 at Eastleigh on 2nd October 1921 with short stove-pipe chimney.  *Author's Collection*

'H15' class No. 490 in later Urie livery.

'H15' class No. 482 on a special passenger working from Waterloo to Bournemouth West via Sway. *Author's Collection*

'H15' class No. 486 photographed near the end of the LSWR's existence. *Stephenson Locomotive Society*

'H15' class No. 486, on test and fitted with indicator shelter, on 11 a.m. Waterloo express (later the 'Atlantic Coast Express') passing Raynes Park in 1920.
*W. H. C. Kelland*
*Bournemouth Railway Club*

| | | |
|---|---|---|
| Cylinders (outside) | 21" x 28" | |
| Bogie wheels | 3' 7" | |
| Coupled wheels | 6' 0" | |
| Wheelbase | 7' 6" + 5' 4½" + 6' 3" + 8' 1" | |
| | = 27' 2½" | |
| Boiler diameter | 5' 6" | |
| Boiler length | 13' 9" (Tubeplates 14½") | |
| Firebox length | 9' 6" | |
| Heating surfaces: | | |
|    Small tubes | 1,252 sq. ft. | |
|    Large tubes | 464 sq. ft. | |
|    Firebox | 168 sq. ft. | |
|    Evaporative total | 1,884 sq. ft. | |
|    Superheater | 308 sq. ft. | |
|    Total | 2,192 sq. ft. | |
| Working pressure | 175 lb | |
| Grate area | 31½ sq. ft. | |
| Weights in working order: | LSWR | Southern (1928) |
|    Bogie | 19T 16C | 21T 5C |
|    Leading coupled wheels | 19T 19C | 20T 7C |
|    Centre coupled wheels | 19T 19C | 20T 9C |
|    Trailing coupled wheels | 19T 18C | 20T 0C |
|    Engine total | 79T 12C | 82T 1C |
|    Tender | 49T 0C | 48T 12C |
|    Engine & Tender | 128T 12C | 130T 13C |

In order to accommodate the Drummond boiler's 9 ft. 6 in. firebox, the wheelbase was 7 in. longer than the 482 series. Although an unimportant difference in itself, unfortunately it also necessitated the grate being long, shallow and virtually flat, thereby making firing extremely difficult, especially with poor quality wartime coal.

For a time No. 335 was stationed at Eastleigh, but by mid-year it had been transferred to Nine Elms and no longer had a regular crew. Nos. 482-91 reacted well to general useage, but No. 335's grate proved the downfall of many firemen. With the former much of the coal could be spread below the door and left to the engine's movement for distribution to the front of the grate, but No. 335

required much more skilful attention. This particularly applied to the front of the grate, which had to be well covered and fiercely burning to maintain full steam pressure and avoid clinkering. As a result, it failed to gain the same acclaim as Nos. 482-91. Over the years it had become recognised South Western practice to banish temperamental or intractable express engines to the larger provincial sheds, in this instance to Salisbury, where, shared by two crews and with some experimentation, the steaming difficulty was largely overcome and, although seldom bettering the performance of Nos. 482-91, No. 335 nevertheless gave long and useful service.

All eleven worked high mileages to the first general repair, details being:

| No. | Date | Mileage | No. | Date | Mileage |
|---|---|---|---|---|---|
| 335 | 10/1917 | 97,694 | 487 | 12/1917 | 137,837 |
| 482 | 9/1920 | 196,426 | 488 | 11/1919 | 178,669 |
| 483 | 7/1920 | 187,645 | 489 | 10/1920 | 187,892 |
| 484 | 12/1919 | 180,913 | 490 | 5/1919 | 169,257 |
| 485 | 3/1920 | 190,247 | 491 | 6/1917 | 116,614 |
| 486 | 3/1921 | 228,971 | | | |

At Grouping all entered Southern Railway stock to be painted Maunsell green and receive the E-prefix, details being:

| | | | | | | | |
|---|---|---|---|---|---|---|---|
| 335 | 12/1923 | 482 | 4/1924 | 483 | 4/1924 | 484 | 11/1926 |
| 485 | 2/1924 | 486 | 9/1924 | 487 | 12/1923* | 488 | 7/1925 |
| 489 | 5/1926 | 490 | 12/1926 | 491 | 5/1925 | | |

* No. 487 was painted goods black in error, this being rectified in February 1927.

Although working regularly to Southampton, Bournemouth, Salisbury and Exeter, 4—6—0s, except for a yearly visit for bridge testing, never appeared at Portsmouth before Grouping. However, in June 1923, 'T14s' commenced appearing on Saturday reliefs and later were joined by 'N15s', 'H15s' and 'S15s', of which only the last mentioned

Lens of Sutton

'H15' class No. 486 repainted in Southern Railway livery and with E-prefix in September 1924.

'H15' class No. 330, rebuilt from Drummond 'F13' class, passing Hewish Gates with a Plymouth express on 2nd August 1928.

H. C. Casserley

'H15' class No. 332 at Exeter Queen Street on a Plymouth express. *Lens of Sutton*

An unusual view of No. 335 showing the rear of the Drummond 'water-cart' tender in early Maunsell livery with E-prefix.

*Author's Collection*

Maunsell 'H15' No. 474 assembled at Eastleigh, using frames, wheels, and valve gear supplied from Ashford and fitted with 'N15' coned boiler.                                                                          *R. C. Riley Collection*

could be relied upon to keep time, the other classes usually dropping 4 or 5 minutes.

No more 'H15s' were built by Urie, but in May 1923 Maunsell authorised the construction of twenty-five, of which ten, Nos. 473-8 and 521-4, were to be new and the remainder rebuilds of Drummond classes 'F13', 'G14' and 'P14'. However, later it was found that so many mixed traffic engines were unnecessary, therefore classes 'G14' and 'P14' were renewed as 'King Arthurs'.

During the war 'F13s' Nos. 330-4 were employed extensively on main line vans, ammunition trains and goods; consequently by Grouping all, except No. 333, superheated in June 1920, required new cylinders and fireboxes. Indeed, No. 334 had been laid aside for this reason in December 1921, therefore its boiler was available to expedite the reconstruction of Nos. 330-3. Details are:

| No. | Laid Aside | Returned to Traffic | Boiler from | Tender from | Cost £ |
|---|---|---|---|---|---|
| 330 | 17/9/1924 | 1/11/1924 | 334 | 331 | 6,310 |
| 331 | 15/2/1924 | 26/11/1924 | 331 | 334 | 6,395 |
| 332 | 13/8/1924 | 11/12/1924 | 333 | 333 | 6,240 |
| 333 | 19/8/1924 | 31/12/1924 | 330 | 332 | 6,225 |
| 334 | 20/12/1921 | 29/1/1925 | 332 | 330 | 6,195 |

Generally the reconstruction followed that of No. 335, but the running plate was straight and they were fitted with Maunsell superheaters, sniffing valves and crosshead vacuum pumps. The smokebox was of the same large diameter pattern as the 482 series, but their attractive Drummond pattern chimney was replaced by a short stove pipe with a capuchon. The tender water capacity was increased to 4,300 gallons by the addition of a well, while

the exhaust steam equipment was removed. The weights in working order were:

| | |
|---|---|
| Bogie | 21T 6C |
| Leading coupled wheels | 19T 16C |
| Centre coupled wheels | 19T 17C |
| Trailing coupled wheels | 19T 12C |
| Engine total | 80T 11C |
| Tender | 49T 3C |
| Engine & Tender | 129T 14C |

On their return to traffic all were sent to join No. 335 at Salisbury, where the long flat grate was expected to prove less troublesome than at other Western Section sheds. Usually employment was on the Salisbury-Exeter passenger and van services, although they were not unknown at Waterloo on semi-fasts and summer Saturday reliefs. Because no spare boiler was available, it was decided to fit No. 332 with a 'King Arthur' pattern boiler in July 1927, but the necessary modifications proved too costly and the scheme was abandoned. As a consequence Nos. 330-5 always spent longer in works than the remainder of the class.

The frames for ten new 'H15s', Nos. 473-8 and 521-4, were cut and machined by Ashford Works in July to November 1923 and with the valve gear, coupled wheels, springing and tender tanks, were despatched to Eastleigh Works for assembly in February to September 1924.

Generally the design followed the '482s', but the 'N15' coned boiler, smokebox and stove-pipe chimney were incorporated, while the running plate was straight without splashers and no tail rods were fitted. All were equipped with Eastleigh superheaters, except No. 524 which had the

'H15' class No. 478 passing Vauxhall on Waterloo to Bournemouth West via Sway passenger train. *Lens of Sutton*

'H15' class No. 522 showing cross-head pump on left-hand side. *Lens of Sutton*

'H15' class No. 522 again, on a Waterloo to Portsmouth via Woking and Guildford train.                    *Lens of Sutton*

'H15' class No. 521 with smokebox snifting valves and Maunsell chimney.                    *Author's Collection*

'H15' class No. 491 carrying Maunsell 'N15' coned boiler, smokebox snifting valves, Ross pop safety valves and smoke deflectors c.1932.
*Author's Collection*

Maunsell pattern and smokebox top snifting valves. Like the 'King Arthurs' and 'S15s', Nos. 823-37, they were fitted with vacuum pumps operated by the left-hand cross-heads. Also, like these classes, the pumps were replaced by ejectors in the 1930s. The tenders were of the Urie double bogie 5,000 gallon pattern. The dimensions were as follows:

| | | |
|---|---|---|
| Cylinders, bogie, coupled wheels and wheelbase | As Nos. 482-91 | |
| Boiler | As 'N15' class | |
| | (No. 524 Maunsell superheater 337 sq. ft.) | |

Weights in working order:

| | Nos. 473-8, 521-3 | No. 524 |
|---|---|---|
| Bogie | 21T 2C | 20T 6C |
| Leading coupled wheels | 19T 14C | 19T 10C |
| Centre coupled wheels | 19T 16C | 19T 14C |
| Trailing coupled wheels | 19T 7C | 19T 8C |
| Engine total | 79T 19C | 78T 18C |
| Tender | 56T 8C | 56T 8C |
| Engine & Tender | 136T 7C | 135T 6C |

Costs: Nos. 473-7 £6,800; No. 478 £6,765; Nos. 521-3 £6,760; No. 524 £6,680.

In January 1925 the allocation was: Nine Elms Nos. 473-7/82-91; Salisbury Nos. 330-5; Bournemouth Nos. 478, 521-4. The last mentioned were the first superheated 4–6–0s shedded at Bournemouth and much was expected of them, but unfortunately they proved a great disappointment as their performance on the Waterloo expresses was much inferior to the Drummond 'D15s'. As a result, on summer Saturdays in 1924-5, Bournemouth regularly borrowed Urie 'S15s' for the Waterloo services, leaving the Oxford through trains to the 'H15s', while in September 1925, following the delivery of 'Scotchmen' Nos. 783-92, these engines were transferred to Eastleigh for less arduous mixed traffic duties.

By 1927 several fireboxes of the '482' series were falling due for renewal and consideration had to be given to the provision of a spare boiler. Luckily, unlike Nos. 330-5, the coned 'N15' pattern could be accommodated with only minor modification; consequently in June 1927 No. 491 was given a boiler of this type. It had been built at Eastleigh Works to Order E121 ('King Arthurs' Nos. 793-806) and therefore No. 491 returned to traffic with a Maunsell chimney, blast-pipe and superheater, smokebox snifting valves, Ross pop safety valves and a 200 lb working pressure. The weights in working order were:

| | |
|---|---|
| Bogie | 21T 2C |
| Leading coupled wheels | 19T 14C |
| Centre coupled wheels | 19T 16C |
| Trailing coupled wheels | 19T 7C |
| Total | 79T 19C |

This type of boiler was retained until withdrawal and gained No. 491 an excellent reputation. The discarded parallel boiler was repaired and used as a spare for Nos. 482-90. Nos. 473-8 and 521-4 were built with 'N15' boilers for which spares of either Urie or Maunsell variety were readily available. At one time or another all this series, except No. 523, carried Maunsell boilers.

With the 1925 summer timetable the loadings of the Continental expresses via Tonbridge were raised from 300 to 425 tons, while North British-built 'King Arthurs' Nos. 763-72 replaced the 4–4–0s of class 'D1' and 'E1'. Unfortunately, because of poor boiler construction, their performance was much inferior to that of Eastleigh-built Nos. 448-57, with time being lost regularly in the London area and with up trains on the banks between Tonbridge and Orpington. The 'Lord Nelson' class was intended for these services, but until these more powerful four-cylinder engines became available, or the 'Scotchmen's' performance could be improved, assistance was required. With this in mind Maunsell decided to give trials to one of the final 'H15s' to ascertain whether the smaller coupled wheels would be advantageous climbing the banks; thus in February 1927 No. 478 was transferred to Battersea and set to work on the Victoria-Dover Marine Continentals. Any Bournemouth crew could have foretold the outcome and time proved them right, for the performance on the banks

'H15' class No. 484 in post-1931 Maunsell livery with a fitted goods train from Feltham yard nearing Byfleet.                         *F. Foote*

was inferior and time was lost consistently between Tonbridge and Ashford. As a result, its stay on the Eastern Section was brief.

Around the same period smoke deflector plates were fitted, the Eastleigh, Schmidt and Robinson superheaters replaced by the Maunsell pattern and various chimney changes made, while after mid-1931 the E-prefix was discarded. Details are:

| No. | Smoke Deflectors | Maunsell Superheater | E-prefix Discarded | Short Flared Chimney |
|---|---|---|---|---|
| 330 | 1/1932 | From new | 1/1932 | 4/1952 |
| 331 | 12/1929 | ,, ,, | 11/1931 | 10/1941 |
| 332 | 1/1930 | ,, ,, | 9/1932 | 5/1947 |
| 333 | 1/1931 | ,, ,, | 11/1932 | 11/1952 |
| 334 | 3/1930 | ,, ,, | 11/1932 | 2/1953 |
| 335 | 12/1930 | 12/1927 | 9/1932 | 1/1952 |

Nos. 330-4 were built with short stove-pipe chimneys, but No. 335 was fitted with a Drummond pattern chimney similar to Nos. 482-91.

| No. | Smoke Deflectors | Maunsell Superheater | E-prefix Discarded | King Arthur Chimney |
|---|---|---|---|---|
| 473 | 11/1931 | 11/1931 | 11/1931 | 6/1927 |
| 474 | 6/1931 | 6/1931 | 6/1931 | 6/1931 |
| 475 | 6/1930 | 6/1930 | 7/1932 | 6/1930 |
| 476 | 1/1931 | 1/1929 | 12/1932 | 1/1929 |
| 477 | 12/1929 | 12/1929 | 9/1931 | 9/1931 |
| 478 | 4/1932 | 5/1930 | 4/1932 | 8/1928 |
| 521 | 4/1931 | 9/1929 | 9/1931 | 7/1927 |
| 522 | 1/1930 | 9/1929 | 4/1932 | 9/1929 |
| 523 | 4/1927 | 7/1927 | 11/1931 | 4/1927 |
| 524 | 4/1930 | From new | 3/1932 | 3/1928 |

All built with 'N15' class stove-pipe chimneys.

| No. | Smoke Deflectors | Maunsell Superheater | E-prefix Discarded | Short Flared Chimney |
|---|---|---|---|---|
| 482 | 3/1932 | 10/1934 | 3/1932 | 3/1932 |
| 483 | 10/1931 | 9/1929 | 4/1934 | 11/1943 (c) |
| 484 | 1/1931 | 1/1931 | 12/1931 | 6/1934 |
| 485 | 8/1930 | 9/1928 (a) | 10/1932 | 10/1932 |
| 486 | 3/1932 | 2/1930 | 3/1932 | 3/1932 |
| 487 | 8/1931 | 5/1929 | 8/1931 | 5/1935 |
| 488 | 12/1929 | 3/1928 | 3/1933 | 7/1939 (d) |
| 489 | 12/1929 | 3/1932 (b) | 3/1932 | 3/1932 |
| 490 | 8/1931 | 5/1929 | 8/1931 | 2/1936 |
| 491 | 11/1931 | 6/1927 | 11/1931 | — (e) |

(a) No. 485 reverted to a Schmidt superheater in 8/1933, the Maunsell pattern being refitted in 8/1935. (b) No. 489 had its Robinson superheater replaced by the Schmidt pattern in 12/1929, before receiving the Maunsell type in 3/1932. (c) No. 483 carried a '473' series stove-pipe chimney from 4/1924 to 11/1943. (d) No. 488 carried a '330' series stove-pipe chimney from 7/1925 to 7/1939. (e) No. 491 carried a '330' series stove-pipe chimney from 10/1917 to 6/1927, when a 'King Arthur' pattern chimney was fitted.

The replacement chimneys fitted to Nos. 482-90 in 1932-43 were similar to those originally carried by the 'Lord Nelson' class.

In June 1935 Nos. 330/1/3 were transferred from Salisbury to Nine Elms for the ocean liner specials and Bournemouth excursions, but as substitutes for the 'T14' class they were not appreciated by the London crews and in the autumn returned to Salisbury. Nos. 476/7 were transferred to Eastleigh in January 1936, but otherwise shed changes were rare with the allocation and duties in mid-1939 being:

| Shed | Allocation | Duties |
|---|---|---|
| Nine Elms | 473/4/82-91 | There were 7 weekday duties: Nos. 4 and 8 covered Waterloo-Salisbury semi-fasts by day and Salisbury-Nine Elms Yard fast goods at night; No. 92 goods to Fratton, passenger to Eastleigh and goods to Nine Elms Yard. Nos. 93/4 two duties covering goods to Dorchester, Weymouth-Bournemouth semi-fasts and Dorchester-Nine Elms Yard goods; No. 95 Waterloo-Southampton docks vans, returning on a goods; No. 98 goods Nine Elms Yard-Salisbury and return. |
| Eastleigh | 476-8, 521-4 | One booked duty only: Goods to Salisbury and return. On most days there were passenger, van and goods specials from Southampton docks to London. |
| Salisbury | 330-5, 475 | There were 4 booked weekday duties: No. 473 local passenger services to Eastleigh and Basingstoke by day and Salisbury-Nine Elms Yard goods by night; No. 448 Waterloo semi-fasts and Salisbury-Basingstoke goods; No. 464 Salisbury-Eastleigh-Southampton goods; No. 485 Salisbury-Exmouth Junction goods and Sidmouth Junction-Salisbury milk tankers. |

On summer Saturdays there were additional duties, although these had acquired the 'next-best-thing' status for they were booked as 'N15' or 'H15', implying the former where possible, but if not an 'H15' would have to do.

The Bulleid livery changes first affected the class in late 1938, details being:

Maunsell green, black and white lining, Bulleid lettering, cabside numerals: Nos. 475/86 (November 1938), 473, 524 (December 1938), No. 330 (February 1939).

Olive green, green and yellow lining, Bulleid lettering, cabside numerals: Nos. 332, 491 (May 1939).

Olive green, black and yellow lining, Bulleid lettering, cabside numerals: Nos. 482/8 (July 1939), 485 (August 1939), 477 (September 1939).

Maunsell green, unlined, Bulleid lettering, cabside numerals: Nos. 334, 487 (February 1940), 335 (August 1940), 478 (July 1940), 483/90 (May 1940), 523 (April 1940).

Malachite green, unlined, Bulleid lettering, cabside numerals: Nos. 474/6/89 (October 1940).

All later Southern repaints, commencing with Nos. 475/86, 521 in March 1941, were plain black.

At the outbreak of war, those stationed at Nine Elms and Eastleigh were transferred to the Southampton Docks troop, van and goods specials, while in October 1940 a re-allocation of the class took Nos. 333, 484/6, 524 to Feltham and No. 521 to Bournemouth for main line goods service. In August 1941 the class was passed for working as far east as Chichester and at once Eastleigh and Salisbury engines commenced appearing daily on van trains and goods. One, No. 521, worked an empty carriage stock train from Eastleigh to Lancing Carriage Works in October 1941, but this is the only known use of the class before 1946, when several appearances occurred yearly.

'H15' class No. 488 with '330' series stove-pipe chimney and smoke deflectors but still retaining the E-prefix. *Author's Collection*

'H15' class No. 334 at Waterloo on a West of England express in the mid-1930s.

P. Ransome Wallis

'H15' class No. 332 at Southampton Town Quay in the late 1930s.

*N. Shepherd, cty. R. C. Riley*

'H15' class No. 334 with smoke deflectors but retaining crosshead pump.

*R. C. Riley Collection*

A splendid view of 'H15' class No. 475 with 'King Arthur' chimney and in post-1931 Maunsell livery at Basingstoke in 1936.

*H. E. Simmonds*

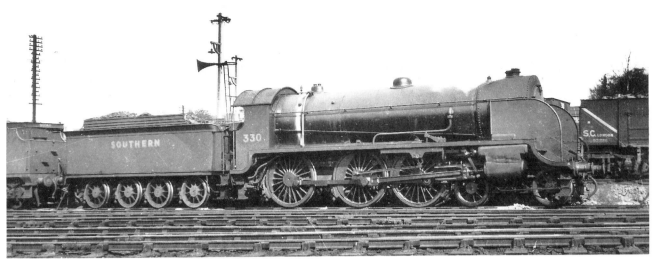

'H15' class No. 330 in wartime black livery at Salisbury on 26th September 1946.                    *R. C. Riley*

No. 478 was loaned to the Great Western in November-December 1941, being stationed at Old Oak Common and employed on London area goods. At the time 'S15s' Nos. 496-9 and 'N15Xs' Nos. 2327-32 had been transferred on loan to the Great Western and No. 478 was substituting for No. 2330, which was under repair at Eastleigh Works. On being returned, it was borrowed for several weeks by Basingstoke and employed on the Portsmouth services via Eastleigh and several troop specials.

In mid-1942, after general repairs, No. 524 was on loan to Bournemouth, while Nos. 333/5 were transferred to Eastleigh in January 1943, but otherwise little of note occurred before March 1944, when the arrival of War Department 2—8—0s Nos. 7436-45 at Eastleigh permitted the transfer of Nos. 477, 522/3 to Nine Elms, No. 478 to Feltham and Nos. 333/5, 476 to Salisbury.

When the 2—8—0s were recalled for military service on the Continent between December 1944 and January 1945,

'H15' class No. 488 shortly after repainting in July 1939 in olive green livery with black and yellow lining, Bulleid lettering and cabside numerals.                    *P. Ransome Wallis*

'H15' class No. 30490 in BR mixed traffic livery at Nine Elms on 16th July 1949.    *C. C. B. Herbert*

the 'H15' allocation became: Nine Elms Nos. 477/82-91; Feltham Nos. 473/4/8; Eastleigh Nos. 521-4; Salisbury Nos. 330-5, 475/6. After VE Day, it was not long before the ocean liner specials recommenced running, with No. 486 and 'S15' No. 837 working those for RMS *Queen Mary* on 11th August 1945.

All entered British Railways stock at Nationalisation to be renumbered into the 30,000 series and from October 1948 receive the lined black secondary passenger livery. Two carried the temporary S-prefix, No. S335 from 6th March to 27th November 1948 and No. S482 from 14th February 1948 to 24th November 1950, while the early repaints were plain black. Details are:

| | | | | | |
|---|---|---|---|---|---|
| S482 | 2/1948 | 30330 | 9/1948 | 30334 | 6/1948 |
| 30475 | 10/1948 | 30476 | 6/1948 | 30477 | 9/1948 |
| 30485 | 7/1948 | 30486 | 9/1948 | 30489 | 5/1948 |

Around this period the smokebox snifting valves were removed and these dates, together with those of renumbering and being painted lined black, are:

| No. | BR No. | Lined Black Livery | Snifting Valves Removed |
|---|---|---|---|
| 330 | 9/1948 | 4/1952 | 9/1948 |
| 331 | 3/1949 | 5/1951 | 5/1951 |
| 332 | 5/1949 | 5/1949 | 5/1949 |
| 333 | 10/1948 | 12/1949 | 9/1947 |
| 334 | 6/1948 | 2/1953 | 6/1948 |
| 335 | 11/1948 | 11/1948 | 11/1948 |
| 473 | 1/1950 | 1/1950 | 1/1950 |
| 474 | 2/1949 | 9/1951 | 2/1949 |
| 475 | 10/1948 | 10/1952 | 10/1948 |
| 476 | 6/1948 | 8/1951 | 6/1948 |
| 477 | 9/1948 | 11/1952 (a) | 9/1948 |
| 478 | 12/1948 | 12/1948 | 4/1948 |
| 482 | 11/1950 | 11/1950 | 2/1948 |
| 483 | 8/1950 | 8/1950 | 11/1947 |
| 484 | 10/1948 | 10/1948 | 10/1948 |
| 485 | 7/1948 | 1/1951 | 7/1948 |
| 486 | 9/1948 | 9/1951 | 9/1948 |
| 487 | 6/1948 | 7/1949 | 6/1947 |
| 488 | 2/1949 | 2/1949 | 2/1949 |
| 489 | 5/1948 | 9/1950 | 5/1948 |
| 490 | 11/1948 | 11/1948 | 11/1948 |
| 491 | 3/1949 | 9/1950 (a) | 12/1947 |
| 521 | 6/1948 | 6/1949 | 6/1949 |
| 522 | 1/1949 | 1/1953 | 1/1949 |
| 523 | 6/1948 | 7/1949 | 6/1948 |
| 524 | 1/1949 | 12/1952 | 10/1950 |

(a) Nos. 30477 and 30491 were erroneously painted plain black in 5/1951 and 3/1949, this being remedied in 11/1952 and 9/1950.

When recently applied or well cleaned, the lined black suited the class extremely well, probably better than Maunsell green.

Despite a large allocation of Pacifics, 'Lord Nelsons' and 'King Arthurs', Nine Elms still found it necessary on summer Saturdays to employ the class on the Bournemouth reliefs and ocean liner specials. Indeed, Nos. 30334/5 were transferred from Salisbury for this purpose in May 1950 and rostered regularly on the 7.48 a.m. Wimbledon-Bournemouth Central and the 9.54 a.m. Waterloo-Bournemouth West, returning with the 12.30 p.m. and 3.18 p.m. respectively, while Nos. 30476/84/5/8/90 shared the Waterloo-Basingstoke-Salisbury semi-fasts and Nos. 30330/2/3 gave spirited performances on up West of England reliefs. Less use was made of the class in the following summer, although No. 30483 successfully replaced a failed diesel on 11.30 a.m. Weymouth-Waterloo, but in the 1952 summer with the absence of main line diesels, the demand for their services returned and regular appearances were made on the 10.42 a.m. and 12.54 p.m. down Bournemouths and the 9.27 a.m. Wimbledon.

Around this period a number of tender changes occurred, including:

| No. | Date | Tender from |
|---|---|---|
| 30482 | 11/1854 | 'S15' No. 498 |
| 30484 | 1/1955 | 'S15' No. 30502 |
| 30488 | 4/1954 | 'N15' No. 30754 |

'H15' class No. 30490 again in BR mixed traffic livery but with early design totem on the tender. *Author*

'H15' class No. 30483 at Eastleigh shortly after repainting in 1950. *W. Gilbert*

'H15' class No. 30485 leaving Basingstoke with a down fitted goods train in the early 1950s.

P. Ransome Wallis

'H15' class No. 30331 circa 1951. *Author's Collection*

'H15' class No. 30477 at Eastleigh on 15th June 1953. *Author*

'H15' class No. 30335, the rebuild of Drummond 'E14', in the early 1950s.     *L. Elsey*

'H15' class No. 30485 at Eastleigh on 2nd June 1951.     *Author*

'H15' class No. 30486 at Eastleigh. It was withdrawn from service in July 1959.
*Photomatic*

All were of the Urie 5,000 gallon pattern.

Nos. 30485/90 were condemned in April and June 1955, with Nos. 30330/2, 30483/7 following in 1956-7, although this did not predict general withdrawal for during the same period Nos. 30331, 30486/9/91, 30521/3/4 received heavy repairs. Unexpectedly at this late date No. 30524 was repaired at Brighton instead of Eastleigh Works. Equally, if not more, unexpected was the appearance of No. 30476 at Canterbury West on 10th August 1958 at the head of a troop special from Portsmouth, routed via Clapham Junction, Orpington and Tonbridge. Its arrival at Ashford MPD for servicing caused such a sensation that a month was spent rusticating at the back of the shed before official permission was granted for its return home light engine over the same route with a speed restriction of 30 mph. Four months later, on 4th January 1959, it trespassed again by working from Lancing to Haywards Heath to collect two damaged diesel sets for repair at Eastleigh Carriage Works.

In anticipation of the Kent Coast electrification releasing more Pacifics, BR standard 4–6–0s, 'King Arthurs' and 'Schools' to the Western Section, general repairs ceased with No. 30522 in March 1959, while Nos. 30473/7/8/82/4/6/8 were condemned as heavy attention became necessary. This left only ten in service, Nos. 30331, 30522-4 at Salisbury, Nos. 30474-6 at Eastleigh and Nos. 30489/91, 30521 at Nine Elms for which there were only three booked duties, two at Salisbury and one at Eastleigh. The former covered two loaded ballast hopper trains to Woking and return, with lengthy periods in between on Guildford shed, while the Eastleigh duty involved the 1.21 a.m. goods to Southampton Docks, the 3.55 a.m. Bevois Park sidings-Salisbury goods, the 7.55 a.m. goods back to Eastleigh, the 5.20 p.m. Eastleigh-Portsmouth passenger, the 7.40 p.m. Fratton-Chichester goods and the 11.30 p.m. Chichester-Eastleigh cement train. This was a duty which could not be worked by the same engine on consecutive days, so two Eastleigh 'H15s' were required, with the third usually being employed as shed and coal road pilot. No. 30331 failed at Guildford with leaking tubes on 12th January 1960 and was sent to Redhill shed for attention. Before returning to Guildford on 23rd January, it

worked an empty wagon train to Tonbridge West Yard and returned later in the day tender first.

Further withdrawals occurred until by mid-1961 only Nos. 30475/6 and 30521-3 remained in stock, spasmodically working goods and ballast trains. All had gone by the end of the year, the last reported in traffic being No. 30523 standing on a van train at Salisbury on 6th December 1961.

## ENGINE SUMMARY

| No. | Date | Order No. | Maunsell Superheater | | Mileage | Withdrawn |
|---|---|---|---|---|---|---|
| 330 | 11/1924 | A17 | When built | | 1,043,516 | 5/1957 |
| 331 | ” | ” | ” | ” | 1,149,690 | 3/1961 |
| 332 | 12/1924 | ” | ” | ” | 968,484 | 11/1956 |
| 333 | ” | ” | ” | ” | 1,064,166 | 10/1958 |
| 334 | 1/1925 | ” | ” | ” | 1,028,883 | 6/1958 |
| 335 | 12/1914 | 335 | 12/1927 | | 1,327,650 | 6/1959 |
| 473 | 2/1924 | R16 | 11/1931 | | 1,182,612 | 8/1959 |
| 474 | ” | ” | 6/1931 | | 1,115,567 | 4/1960 |
| 475 | 3/1924 | ” | 6/1930 | | 1,309,376 | 12/1961 |
| 476 | 4/1924 | ” | 1/1929 | | 1,263,643 | 12/1961 |
| 477 | 5/1924 | ” | 12/1929 | | 1,020,549 | 7/1959 |
| 478 | 6/1924 | T16 | 5/1930 | | 1,107,597 | 3/1959 |
| 482 | 3/1914 | H15 | 10/1934 | | 1,471,917 | 5/1959 |
| 483 | 4/1914 | H15 | 9/1929 | | 1,467,889 | 6/1957 |
| 484 | 5/1914 | K15 | 1/1931 | | 1,517,013 | 5/1959 |
| 485 | 6/1914 | H15 | 9/1928 | | 1,303,990 | 4/1955 |
| 486 | 1/1914 | ” | 3/1930 | | 1,512,324 | 7/1959 |
| 487 | 2/1914 | ” | 5/1929 | | 1,419,965 | 11/1957 |
| 488 | 4/1914 | K15 | 3/1928 | | 1,500,637 | 4/1959 |
| 489 | 5/1914 | ” | 3/1932 | | 1,521,178 | 1/1961 |
| 490 | 7/1914 | ” | 5/1929 | | 1,397,637 | 6/1955 |
| 491 | 7/1914 | ” | 6/1927 | | 1,539,740 | 2/1961 |
| 521 | 7/1924 | T16 | 9/1929 | | 1,161,139 | 12/1961 |
| 522 | ” | ” | 4/1929 | | 1,093,943 | 9/1961 |
| 523 | 9/1924 | ” | 7/1929 | | 1,063,049 | 12/1961 |
| 524 | ” | ” | When built | | 1,071,335 | 2/1961 |

All built and broken up at Eastleigh Works.

'N15' No. 740 as built with taper boiler, 'Eastleigh' superheater, stove-pipe chimney, Walschaert's valve gear, Drummond pattern cab and Urie 5,000 gallon double bogie tender.

*Photomatic*

'N15' No. 742 with a Waterloo-West of England Express. *Author's Collection*

# 'N15' Class

During the last two hundred years the United Kingdom has often been at war, but before the present century this seldom concerned the general public for the English Channel and the Royal Navy ensured that all the fighting occurred overseas and only directly involved the Armed Forces. At first this also applied to World War I, but by Christmas 1914 the widening of hostilities had encompassed most homes and industries, including Eastleigh Works where shell casings, gun mountings and other articles of war were being manufactured in addition to maintaining the company's locomotive stock. As a result, new construction had to be abandoned after the completion of 'H15' No. 335. However, this did not prevent Urie planning for the future and on 27th January 1916 he sought and obtained authority from the Locomotive Committee for the construction of ten express and five heavy goods 4—6—0s when circumstances permitted.

The first drawings were completed on 24th February 1916 and these were followed by others throughout 1917 and early 1918 until assembly only awaited Government approval. With final victory in France now forseeable, this was granted in mid-year and the necessary material allotted to Eastleigh Works. By working at weekends, assembly was rapid, with the first express 4—6—0 leaving the erecting shop on 31st August 1918 and the last on 19th November 1919. Known as the 'N15s' and numbered 736-45, they had the following dimensions:

| | |
|---|---|
| Cylinders (outside) | 22" x 28" |
| Maximum travel & lap | $5\,1/8$" and 1" |
| Bogie wheels | 3' 7" |
| Coupled wheels | 6' 7" |
| Wheelbase | 7' 6" + 5' 6" + 7' 0" + 7' 6" = 27' 6" |

| | |
|---|---|
| Boiler diameter | 5' $1^3/8$" to 5' $5\frac{3}{4}$" |
| Boiler length | 13' 9" (tubeplates 14' 2") |
| Firebox length | 9' 0" |
| Heating surfaces: | |
|    Small tubes (167 x 2") | 1,252 sq. ft. |
|    Large tubes (24 x 5¼") | 464 sq. ft. |
|    Firebox | 162 sq. ft. |
|    Total evaporative | 1,878 sq. ft. |
|    Superheater | 308 sq. ft. |
|    Total | 2,186 sq. ft. |
| Working pressure | 180 lb |
| Grate area | 30 sq. ft. |

Weights in working order:

| | LSWR (1920) | Southern (1930) |
|---|---|---|
| Bogie | 21T 18C | 22T 0C |
| Leading coupled wheels | 18T 14C | 19T 7C |
| Centre coupled wheels | 19T 0C | 19T 10C |
| Trailing coupled wheels | 18T 5C | 19T 10C |
| Engine total | 77T 17C | 80T 7C |
| Tender | 57T 1C | 57T 1C |
| Engine and Tender | 134T 18C | 137T 8C |

Construction costs:
Nos. 736-40   £6,740 each
Nos. 741-5    £7,765 each

They were robustly constructed, impressive-looking engines having many details common with 'H15s' Nos. 482-91, including the outside cylinders, exposed Walschaerts valve gear, high running plate, Drummond pattern cabs and double bogie tenders. At the time of introduction the 22 in. by 28 in. cylinders were the largest used in this country, while the boilers were the first built by Eastleigh Works with tapered barrels. This was restricted to the leading ring to reduce the smokebox diameter and lower the weight supported by the bogie. Other differences included the

H. C. Casserley

'N15' No. 754, one of the second batch of 'N15s', at Bournemouth on 9th May 1925.

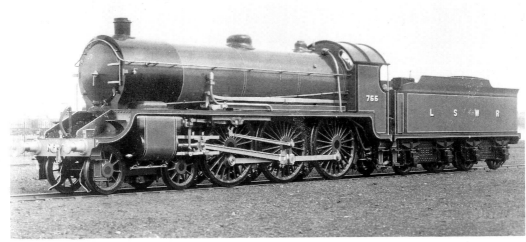

'N15' No. 755 when new in Urie lined green livery.
*Author's Collection*

stark stove-pipe chimney, large dome cover, straight running plate and Eastleigh superheater. The tender was a modified and improved version of that provided for 'H15s' Nos. 482-91 and carried 5,000 gallons of water and 5 tons of coal.

Like the 'H15s', the reciprocating parts were of massive proportions and generously balanced by large and heavy weights at the circumference of the 6 ft. 7 in. coupled wheels. This ensured a smooth and comfortable ride along the track, but also murderously affected the permanent way and underbridges, although this was not appreciated by railway engineers until the findings of the Bridge Stress Committee were published in 1925. Then Eastleigh was duly shocked to discover that the 'H15s', followed closely

'N15' No. 750 at Salisbury on 19th July 1924.

*H. C. Casserley*

'N15' No. 743 with a Waterloo to Plymouth Express at Axminster.
*Author's Collection*

by the 'N15s' and 'S15s', were among the classes having the highest hammer blow in the country. At six revolutions per second, the loadings of the two passenger classes were:

|  | H15 | N15 |
|---|---|---|
| Whole engine | 25.5 tons | 25.5 tons |
| Axle | 10.5 tons | 9.1 tons |
| Wheel | 6.2 tons | 7.3 tons |
| Maximum Combined |  |  |
| Axle | 30.3 tons | 28.6 tons |
| Wheel | 16.1 tons | 17.1 tons |

No. 736 was run-in on the Eastleigh-Bournemouth slows and then used for a series of fuel and haulage trials between Basingstoke and Eastleigh before being despatched to Nine Elms for general service. In those days with little press coverage, few knew of its existence, consequently the appearance of a new 4—6—0 at Waterloo for the 10.50 a.m. West of England express caused a minor sensation. However, the unfortunate passengers undoubtedly viewed the debut with considerably less enthusiasm for 5½ minutes were lost to Basingstoke and 7 more to Salisbury by having to work wrong line round a failed train at Oakley.

Assembly of Nos. 736-40 proceeded to schedule, but Nos. 741-5 were delayed by a shortage of copper and other specialised metals, therefore it was November 1919 before the last entered traffic, when the allocation became: Nine Elms Nos. 736/8-43, Salisbury Nos. 737/44/5. The former had six daily booked duties, four to Salisbury and two to Bournemouth, while Salisbury's Nos. 743-5 had two to Exeter and one to Waterloo.

During the 1921 coal-miners' strike, Nos. 737/9 were converted to oil-burning (Scarab system) and stationed at Nine Elms for working Bournemouth or Salisbury expresses by day and heavy goods by night. No. 739 burst into flames outside Salisbury shed on 28th July 1921 and did

not work again before reconversion to coal-firing. Details are:

| No. | To Oil-burning | To Coal-burning |
|---|---|---|
| 737 | 23/4/1921 | 26/9/1921 |
| 739 | 18/6/1921 | 6/8/1921 |

Ten more, Nos. 746-55, were ordered from Eastleigh Works on 13th October 1921 and delivered between June 1922 and March 1923. The estimated cost was £9,500 each, but, because of falling wages and cheaper materials, the actual costs were: Nos. 746-50 £8,257; 751/2 £7,116; 753-5 £7,354. The original allocation was: Nine Elms Nos. 746-8/51/2; Exmouth Junction Nos. 749/53-5; Salisbury No. 750.

When the class was first introduced the wartime main line speed restriction of 60 mph remained in force and the 10.50 a.m. West of England express was booked 103 minutes for the 83¾ miles non-stop to Salisbury and 105 minutes thence for the 75¾ miles, also non-stop, to Sidmouth Junction, timings which the later Drummond 4—6—0s and the superheated 4—4—0s could maintain with loads of 320 tons. Consequently, the more powerful and heavier 'N15s' were seldom fully extended and most observers had difficulty assessing their performance. However, an extensive track up-grading and relaying programme was underway and by mid-1922 this had encompassed much of the West of England line, thereby permitting not only tighter schedules, but also through engine working, with remanning at Salisbury. Details are:

| Nine Elms: | 10.00 a.m. Waterloo-Exeter | (204 mins) |
|---|---|---|
|  | 4.34 p.m. Exeter-Waterloo | (240 mins) |
|  | 11.00 a.m. Waterloo-Exeter | (204 mins) |
|  | 6.30 p.m. Exeter-Waterloo | (260 mins) |

'N15' No. 737 with its short-lived oil-burning conversion.

*Author's Collection*

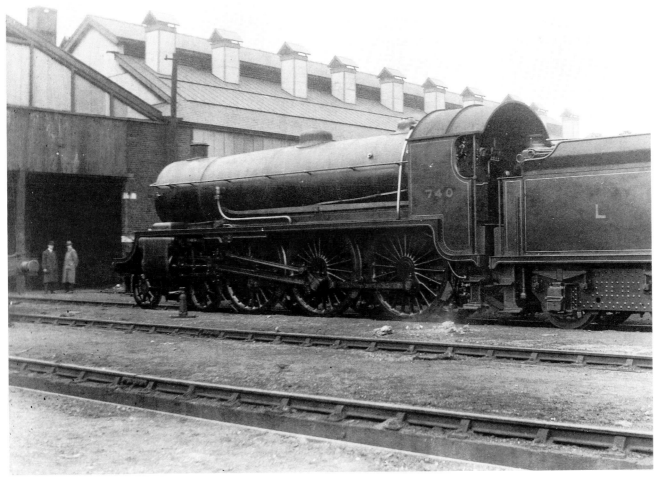

'N15' No. 740 at Nine Elms.

*Collection W. G. Rear*

'N15' No. 739 with a West of England Express.      *Author's Collection*

Exmouth Junction:    10.30 a.m. Exeter-Waterloo   (206 mins)
                   6.00 p.m. Waterloo-Exeter   (247 mins)
                 12.30 p.m. Exeter-Waterloo   (210 mins)
                   9.00 p.m. Waterloo-Exeter   (slow)

Unfortunately, the performance on these through workings was so indifferent that engine-changing at Salisbury was re-introduced in September without waiting for the winter timetable.

At first Urie blamed unenterprising enginemanship for the lackadaisical performance, but following a series of test runs with inspectors on the footplate between Clapham Junction and Salisbury, the allegation had to be withdrawn since the main cause of lost time proved to be poor steaming. Hot coupled wheel boxes also caused trouble, with Nos. 736/8-43/5 all requiring attention by Nine Elms Works on no less than 31 occasions in 1918-22, while later Nos. 736/42/3/5/7 suffered serious frame fracturing. Significantly No. 737/44 of Salisbury avoided both hot boxes and frame fractures. At once remedial measures were introduced, but apart from the provision of a spare set of frames and modifications to the lubricating piping, little had been accomplished before the 31st December 1922, when the South Western ceased to exist.

After Grouping all were painted Maunsell green, received the E-prefix and were named after the characters and places in the Arthurian legends. Details are:

| No. | Southern Livery | Name | Date |
|---|---|---|---|
| 736 | 7/1924 | *Excalibur* | 2/1925 |
| 737 | 10/1925 | *King Uther* | 10/1925 |
| 738 | 5/1924 | *King Pellinore* | 8/1925 |
| 739 | 10/1924 | *King Leodgrance* | 11/1925 |
| 740 | 7/1924 | *Merlin* | 11/1925 |
| 741 | 1/1924 | *Joyous Gard* | 6/1925 |
| 742 | 1/1924 | *Camelot* | 12/1925 |
| 743 | 6/1925 | *Lyonnesse* | 6/1925 |
| 744 | 10/1924 | *Maid of Astolat* | 4/1925 |
| 745 | 9/1924 | *Tintagel* | 4/1925 |
| 746 | 12/1924 | *Pendragon* | 10/1925 |
| 747 | 1/1925 | *Elaine* | 9/1925 |
| 748 | 4/1925 | *Vivien* | 4/1925 |
| 749 | 4/1924 | *Iseult* | 9/1925 |
| 750 | 4/1924 | *Morgan le Fay* | 10/1925 |
| 751 | 4/1924 | *Etarre* | 3/1927 |
| 752 | 12/1924 | *Linette* | 3/1927 |
| 753 | 1/1925 | *Melisande* | 8/1925 |
| 754 | 7/1924 | *The Green Knight* | 9/1925 |
| 755 | 4/1925 | *The Red Knight* | 4/1925 |

On taking office, Maunsell quickly appreciated the N15s' worth, although at the same time realising that some modification was necessary to achieve their full potential. As a result he presented the Eastleigh design staff with

'N15' No. 745 at Salisbury on 30th July 1925, in Maunsell green with tender numerals, E-prefix and named *Tintagel*. *H. C. Casserley*

'N15' No. 755 was named *The Red Knight* when it received Maunsell livery with tender numerals and E-prefix in April 1925.
*Author's Collection*

two related problems, for new construction the incorporation of principles successfully exploited by the Ashford 2–6–0s, and for those already in service, to ascertain by road testing how best to enhance their performance without resorting to costly and extensive reconstruction. Therefore, while Maunsell's personal assistant, J. Clayton, dealt with new construction, the poorest 'N15', No. 742, was taken into Eastleigh Works for fitting with indicating equipment and a smokebox personnel shelter before commencing a series of test runs between Waterloo and Salisbury. Details are:

| Date | Minimum Steam Pressure | Coal Burnt per Mile | Gross Load | Modifications |
|---|---|---|---|---|
| 29/2/1924 | 102 lb/sq. in. | 35.3 lb | 384 tons | As built |
| 1/5/1924 | 120 lb/sq. in. | 32.6 lb | 391 tons | Increased steam and exhaust ports areas, 1/8 in. exhaust clearance. |
| 19/7/1924 | 170 lb/sq. in. | 29.2 lb | 378 tons | As for 1/5/1924, plus a lipped chimney, 5½ in. diameter blast-pipe and 21 in. cylinders. |

On the first test the boiler pressure did not fall below 165 lb per sq. in., while for 75 miles it ranged between 170 and 180 lb, with the indicated horse power exceeding 1000 and occasionally reaching 1200. Further improvement was possible by replacing the valve gear, but the expense was considered prohibitive by the Locomotive Committee, much to the disappointment of the design staff and Running Department.

Eight spare 'King Arthur' class boilers were ordered from the North British Locomotive Company at a cost of £1,450 each on 17th December 1924 and when delivered advantage was taken of their availability to reboiler Nos. 737/42 in October and December 1925. At the same time the former's Urie stove-pipe and No. 742's experimental lipped chimney were replaced by 'King Arthur' class chimneys, while No. 737 also had the area of the steam and exhaust ports increased, the exhaust clearance adjusted to 1/8 in. and the blast-pipe diameter reduced to 5 1/8 in. Both boilers were fitted with Ross pop safety valves working at 200 lb per sq. in., but the smokebox doors and superheaters were of Urie pattern. In 1925-9 'King Arthur' chimneys and the blast-pipe, exhaust clearance and port area modifications were applied to the remainder of the class.

During the 1926 General Strike and the subsequent miners' refusal to return to work, Nos. 737/9 were converted to oil-firing employing equipment stored at Eastleigh Works since 1921. Details are:

| No. | To Oil-burning | Reconverted to Coal-burning | Mileage Worked |
|---|---|---|---|
| 737 | 16/6/1926 | 22/12/1926 | 19,046 |
| 739 | 12/6/1926 | 17/12/1926 | 21,998 |

When first converted to oil-burning, both were stationed at Eastleigh and used on the Southampton Docks-Salisbury goods services, but by mid-July Nine Elms was employing them on the Bournemouth and Salisbury expresses by day and Nine Elms Yard-Southampton Docks goods by night.

On test in August 1926, No. 739's fuel consumption was:

| Route | Load | Fuel Burnt per Train Mile | | |
|---|---|---|---|---|
| | | Oil | Coal | Total |
| Waterloo-Salisbury | 368 tons | 19.3 lb | 13.3 lb | 32.6 lb |
| Salisbury-Waterloo | 341 tons | 17.4 lb | 8.9 lb | 26.3 lb |
| Waterloo-Bournemouth West | 318 tons | 16.6 lb | 9.2 lb | 25.8 lb |
| Bournemouth West-Waterloo | 308 tons | 17.9 lb | 10.1 lb | 28.0 lb |

On a calorific basis approximately 70 per cent of the steam was generated by the oil, which was considered satisfactory, although the percentage was lower than that recorded by 'D15' No. 470, when working the Southampton-Waterloo semi-fasts.

Around this period Eastleigh was experimenting with various chimney and smokebox devices to lift the exhaust gases and steam clear of the boiler top and the cab windows. From these experiments and a series of wind tunnel tests conducted for the Southern by London University, the well-known Maunsell smoke deflector plates were evolved and fitted to all the large Urie and Maunsell passenger and goods tender classes. The dates when these appeared on the 'N15s', together with those for the fitting of 'King Arthur' pattern chimneys, Maunsell superheaters, snifting valves and the removal of the E-prefix, are as follows:

| No. | Smoke Deflectors | 'King Arthur' Chimney | Maunsell Superheater | E-prefix Discarded |
|---|---|---|---|---|
| 736 | 9/1928 | 9/1928 | 9/1930 | 2/1932 |
| 737 | 6/1928 | 10/1925 | 6/1929 | 2/1932 |
| 738 | 7/1928 | 7/1928 | 3/1930 | 10/1932 |
| 739 | 1/1928 | 1/1928 | 5/1930 | 8/1931 |
| 740 | 5/1928 | 1/1927 | 12/1929 | 11/1931 |
| 741 | 1/1928 | 6/1925 | 2/1929 | 9/1932 |
| 742 | 6/1928 | 12/1925 | 8/1930 | 2/1932 |
| 743 | 11/1927 | 6/1925 | 6/1930 | 1/1933 |
| 744 | 11/1927 | 6/1927 | 1/1930 | 1/1932 |
| 745 | 7/1928 | 7/1928 | 1/1932 | 1/1932 |
| 746 | 1/1929 | 1/1929 | 1/1929 | 10/1932 |
| 747 | 8/1928 | 9/1925 (b) | 11/1930 | 6/1932 |
| 748 | 11/1929 | 11/1929 | 11/1929 | 5/1932 |
| 749 | 8/1927 | 9/1925 | 12/1928 | 5/1932 |
| 750 | 1/1928 | 1/1928 | 2/1930 | 11/1931 |
| 751 | 12/1928 | 12/1928 | 6/1929 | 10/1931 |
| 752 | 12/1927 | 12/1928 | 9/1930 | 3/1932 |
| 753 | 1/1928 (a) | 5/1926 | 7/1928 | 9/1931 |
| 754 | 7/1928 | 9/1925 | 1/1930 | 6/1932 |
| 755 | 1/1928 | 7/1927 | 3/1929 | 2/1932 |

(a) No. 753 was fitted experimentally with a strip of curved steel across the smokebox in front of the chimney from 21st May to 16th June 1926. (b) A 'Lord Nelson' class chimney carried from 30th November to 6th December 1937.

In June 1928 the allocation was: Nine Elms Nos. 738/41/2/5/8/50/2/3/5; Bournemouth Nos. 736/43; Salisbury Nos. 739/49/51/4; Exmouth Junction Nos. 737/40/4/6/7. The two stationed at Bournemouth, reputedly poor performers, were mainly employed on the through trains to Oxford, but the other sheds rostered their 'N15s' indiscrim-

'N15' No. 742, the poorest 'N15', with lipped chimney and other modifications carried out during the 1924 trials at Clapham Junction, on 5th May 1925 prior to being reboilered. Note the absence of SR cabside numberplate. *H. C. Casserley*

'N15' No. 753 *Melisande* at Eastleigh with the experimental smoke deflecting plate carried from 21st May to 16th June 1926.
*R. C. Riley Collection*

'N15' No. 748 *Lyonnesse* with smoke deflectors and 'King Arthur' chimney on a down express of GWR stock passing through the former Blechynden station before entering Southampton West.

*L & GRP, cty. David & Charles*

inately with the 'King Arthurs'. In early 1929 Nos. 737/53 were transferred to Eastleigh to replace 'H15s' on that shed's two Bournemouth-Waterloo turns.

With their more advanced front-end, the 'King Arthurs' undoubtedly were better engines, but nevertheless many Salisbury and Exmouth Junction crews preferred the older engines for the undulating West of England line, where their superior work on the banks could be fully exploited. From Waterloo to Basingstoke the continuous collar work often drained the Urie boiler, forcing drivers to ease the cut-off and lose time. West of Salisbury this seldom occurred for the intermingling of gradients allowed the short banks to be rushed while those of longer duration could be resolutely attacked with little fear of any steam loss inhibiting later progress. Once over the summit, the following descent offered firemen ample scope to rally the fire in preparation for the next climb — a driving pattern designed for the 'N15s' for it promoted their ability to pound away on the banks and concealed any shortcomings on the flat.

In 1929-30 a friend of the author commuted daily between Salisbury and Exeter, details of his journeys are:

| Class | No. of Journeys | Average Load tons | Semley mph | Sherborne mph | Average Speeds Crewkerne mph | Axminster mph | Honiton Summit mph |
|---|---|---|---|---|---|---|---|
| N15 | 37 | 321 | 50½ | 79 | 77½ | 82 | 37 |
| King Arthur | 31 | 336 | 53½ | 81 | 79½ | 85 | 35½ |
| S15 (Maunsell) | 19 | 308 | 48 | 71 | 70½ | 73½ | 37 |
| H15 (330 series) | 13 | 289 | 45 | 69½ | 67 | 68½ | 25½ |
| N (2–6–0) | 6 | 247 | 48 | 70 | 65 | 69 | 31 |
| Lord Nelson | 2 | 340 | 51 | 83 | 75 | 87 | 35 |
| T14 | 1 | 276 | 39 | 69 | 66 | 71 | 20½ |
| T9 | 14 | 238 | 41 | 74 | 73 | 79½ | 23 |

The highest speeds recorded near Axminster were:

| | |
|---|---|
| N15 (No. 754 *The Green Knight*) | 86 mph |
| King Arthur (No. 449 *Sir Torre*) | 90 mph |
| S15 (No. 826) | 84 mph |
| T9 (No. 717) | 91 mph |

At this period most 'N15s' retained 22 in. Urie cylinders, but all renewals were 21 in. and when this occurred most drivers considered that the performance climbing the West of England banks had diminished. Dates of renewal are:

Urie pattern (21 in.): Nos. 736 – 8/1924, 737 – 6/1928, 738 – 3/1930, 739 – 10/1928, 740 – 12/1929, 741 – 2/1929, 744 – 6/1927, 746 – 1/1929, 751 – 2/1930.

Maunsell pattern (double exhaust ports): Nos. 740 – 1/1934, 742 – 8/1930, 743 – 6/1930, 745 – 5/1930, 747 – 3/1933, 748 – 5/1931, 749 – 3/1931, 752 – 9/1930, 754 – 6/1932.

Bulleid pattern: Nos. 738 – 4/1939, 750 – 4/1941, 751 – 5/1941, 755 – 2/1940.

It was the combination of Bulleid cylinders and a Lemaître multi-blast-pipe, which so rejuvenated No. 755 *The Red Knight* in 1940-5 that Nine Elms regularly rostered it for 'Lord Nelson' duties. Undoubtedly, the performance on the banks was adversely affected by the smaller cylinders, but otherwise, like the earlier blast-pipe and motion modifications, they proved beneficial, therefore it is surprising that the use of 'King Arthur' boilers had virtually no impact. Indeed, Eastleigh crews always preferred those carrying Urie boilers. Nevertheless, at one time or another, all except Nos. 749/55 ran with the 'King Arthur' pattern, Nos. 736/7/40/3/5/8/53 on three occasions.

'N15' No. 751 *Etarre* at Eastleigh with 'King Arthur' boiler and smoke deflectors.          *R. S. Carpenter Collection*

In the 1930s the annual mileages, like those of the 'King Arthurs', were high and indicate the extensive use made of the class, details being:

|  |  |  | *Miles* |
|---|---|---|---|
| 1931-3 | Nine Elms | (Nos. 738/9/41/2/5/8/50/2) | 45,900 |
|  | Salisbury | (Nos. 749/51/4) | 42,000 |
|  | Exmouth Junction | (Nos. 740/3/4/6/7) | 47,000 |
|  | Bournemouth | (No. 736) | 43,000 |
|  | Eastleigh | (Nos. 737/53/5) | 39,000 |
| 1935-9 | Nine Elms | (Nos. 736-42) | 42,600 |
|  | Salisbury | (Nos. 747/8) | 37,800 |
|  | Exmouth Junction | (Nos. 743/4) | 43,200 |
|  | Eastleigh | (Nos. 749-55) | 36,100 |
|  | Bournemouth/Salisbury | (Nos. 745/6) | 48,600 |

The original scheduled mileage between general repairs was 70,000, but this was increased to 85,000 in 1936. Details for No. 755 *The Red Knight* are:

| *General Repair* | *Dates in Works* | | *Mileage* | *New* |
|---|---|---|---|---|
|  | *From* | *To* |  | *28/3/1923* |
| 1st | 29/12/1924 | 9/4/1925 | 66,584 |  |
| 2nd | 21/4/1927 | 9/7/1927 | 75,044 |  |
| 3rd | 8/1/1929 | 7/3/1929 | 67,275 |  |
| 4th | 4/10/1930 | 15/11/1930 | 61,297 |  |
| 5th | 12/1/1932 | 13/2/1932 | 55,551 |  |
| 6th | 11/8/1933 | 12/9/1933 | 73,582 |  |
| 7th | 4/7/1935 | 17/8/1935 | 91,956 |  |
| 8th | 7/12/1936 | 16/1/1937 | 73,160 |  |
| 9th | 9/12/1939 | 14/2/1940 | 95,156 |  |
| 10th | 26/6/1942 | 5/8/1942 | 86,014 |  |
| 11th | 31/7/1944 | 13/9/1944 | 105,340 |  |
| 12th | 21/6/1947 | 2/8/1947 | 125,322 |  |
| 13th | 13/9/1949 | 21/10/1949 | 92,198 |  |
| 14th | 27/11/1951 | 29/12/1951 | 62,913 |  |
| 15th | 1/9/1955 | 24/9/1955 | 141,734 |  |
| To withdrawal 11/5/1957 |  |  | 57,148 |  |
| Total mileage |  |  | 1,330,274 |  |
| Average yearly mileage |  |  | 39,126 |  |
| Average mileage between general repairs |  |  | 84,875 |  |

The average repair mileages for the 'N15s', 'King Arthurs', 'Schools', 'Lord Nelsons', 'N15Xs' and 'H15s' in 1933-9 were:

| *Class* | *General to Intermediate Repair* | | *Between General Repairs* | |
|---|---|---|---|---|
|  | *Miles* | *Months* | *Miles* | *Months* |
| N15 | 52,815 | 14.1 | 85,269 | 22.1 |
| King Arthur | 54,858 | 15.1 | 84,546 | 21.3 |
| Schools | 44,755 | 13.6 | 90,339 | 25.8 |
| Lord Nelson | 54,019 | 14.1 | 88,902 | 24.6 |
| N15X | 37,968 | 12.8 | 87,405 | 27.8 |
| H15 | 39,836 | 12.2 | 85,457 | 26.1 |

These figures are taken from a report presented by Bulleid in July 1939, but the mileages do not agree entirely with those recorded by the engine cards.

The maintenance examination periods for the 'N15s' in 1936-9 were:

10-14 days: Wash out boiler, examine all accessible parts of the boiler, including waterways, tubes, ashpan, firebox and smokebox.

Monthly: Boiler water gauges, driver's brake valve, vacuum limit and drip-valves, cylinder draincocks and gear, steam heating equipment (winter months) and manifold stopcock.

Two-monthly: Live and exhaust steam injectors, clackboxes, vacuum and hand brakes, and lubricators.

Three-monthly: Test safety valves and pressure gauges and renew firebox fusible plugs.

Six-monthly: Measure and record tyre profiles and thickness, and examine main frames, wheels and tender.

12,500 miles: Examine in position the connecting rods and big-ends, coupling rods, crossheads, axles, valve gear, reverser, drawgear, bogie, buffers and springs. Withdraw underfeed journal pads of all axle boxes.

25,000 miles: Dismantle and examine the connecting rods and big-ends, coupling rods, crank pins and crossheads. Withdraw valves and pistons, renew rings, decarbonise ports and steam passages and check cylinder relief valves, draincocks etc. Brake shoes to be replaced if necessary.

Annually: Boiler examined by H.O. boiler inspector with tubes withdrawn as directed.

The 'N15' boiler was trouble-free, but because of excessive weight, motion wear was extensive, while the thrust of the two outside cylinders severely punished the axleboxes and led to rough riding after 25,000 miles. Unlike the 'Schools' and 'Lord Nelsons', the axlebox guides were not provided with hornblock wedges, an omission arising from Urie's fear that a maladjusted wedge could cause an axlebox to lock in its guide and cause a derailment.

In 1938 Bulleid was considering replacing the Maunsell dark green of the express classes with a brighter and more attractive livery and in April 1939 had No. 749 *Iseult* experimentally painted bright green with cabside numerals and black cylinders. The left-hand side was without lining, but on the other side the boiler bands were painted black. The rear of the tender was plain black, with the left-hand sidesheets carrying standard Southern lettering and on the right-hand the initials 'SR' in large block capitals. Apparently the directors were not impressed by either livery for in June 1938 the same engine was painted light (malachite) green, with black and white lining, green cylinders and 'Southern' inscribed across both sides of the tender in lined block lettering. On one side the numerals were painted on the black smoke deflector plates and on the other the cab sidesheets. No. 749 *Iseult* was returned to traffic in standard Maunsell livery on 8th July 1938, but the final experimental livery formed the basis of the style introduced on the 'Schools' class working from Bournemouth later in the month.

These livery changes first affected the 'N15s' towards the end of the year, details being:

Maunsell green, black and white lining, Bulleid lettering, cabside numerals: Nos. 748 (November 1938), 736 (December 1938), 751 (January 1939), 743/54 (February 1939), 752 (March 1939), 737/8 (April 1939).

Olive green, green and yellow lining, Bulleid lettering, cabside numerals: No. 745 (April 1939).

Olive green, black and yellow lining, Bulleid lettering, cabside numerals: Nos. 742 (June 1939), 753 (July 1939), 740/4 (Novem-

'N15' No. 737 *King Uther* at Pokesdown on 25th September 1943, with 'King Arthur' boiler, fitted with multiple blast-pipes and large diameter chimney.
*C. L. Caddy Collection*

ber 1939), 747/55 (February 1940), 741 (April 1940), 736 (May 1940).

Malachite green, black and white lining, Bulleid lettering, cabside numerals: No. 746 (March 1939).

Malachite green, black and yellow lining, Bulleid lettering, cabside numerals: Nos. 737/9 (July 1940), 750 (April 1941), 743/51 (May 1941), 745 (June 1941), 746/8 (July 1941), 754 (October 1941), 744 (March 1942).

*Non-standard repaints:*

Maunsell green, green and yellow lining, Bulleid lettering, cabside numerals: Nos. 749 (September 1940), 752 (February 1941).

Malachite green, unlined, Bulleid lettering, cabside numerals: No. 738 (May 1941).

All later repaints until April 1946, commencing with No. 742 in June 1942, were plain black.

A Lemaître blast-pipe, large diameter pre-fabricated chimney and Bulleid pattern 21 in. cylinders were fitted to No. 755 *The Red Knight* in February 1940. This engine had always been a good 'N15', but now it not only completely outstripped the remainder of the class, but also the 'King Arthurs' and 'Lord Nelsons'. News of this rejuvenation must have reached the ears of the Nine Elms shedmaster for within weeks of being released by Eastleigh Works, he had successfully negotiated a transfer. Four others were similarly fitted with multiple blast pipes and large diameter chimneys, their details being:

736 12/1940    737 2/1941    741 12/1940    752 2/1941

Nos. 738/43/5/6/8 were also scheduled for conversion, but this was cancelled in April 1941 because of the shortage of labour and materials. No. 743 was actually fitted with a Lemaitre blast-pipe, but as the smokebox had not been cut and a large diameter chimney provided, it was removed. In regular service Nos. 736/7/41/52 performed better than the standard 'N15s', but were outclassed by No. 755. The

smoke deflectors were retained, but, because of the softer blast, were less effective and drivers complained of smoke obscuring their look-out. As a result, Nos. 736/52/5 had the top section of the plates adjusted to vertical in November, March and January 1945. No significant improvement occurred, so the modification was not applied to Nos. 737/41.

The September 1939 allocation was Nine Elms Nos. 736-42, Salisbury Nos. 745-8, Exmouth Junction Nos. 743/4 and Eastleigh Nos. 749-55, but the war caused several early transfers, including Nos. 741/2 to Eastleigh in exchange for 'H15s' Nos. 521/4 sent to Bournemouth and Feltham for main line goods duty. In February 1940 Eastleigh lost Lemaitre-fitted No. 755 to Nine Elms and received No. 740 in exchange, but otherwise the Eastleigh allocation remained constant until November 1940, when the loss of several Maunsell 'Q' class 0—6—0s and more mixed traffic 'H15s' was again made good by further 'N15' transfers which raised the total to twelve, Nos. 739/40/2/4/7-54. They had to cover ten booked duties, all main line goods or vans, except a Bournemouth West-Waterloo semi-fast and an Eastleigh-Bournemouth-Weymouth slow. One of the goods duties reached Exmouth Junction, this commenced with coal empties from Bevois Park sidings to Salisbury, where a Feltham 'S15' was relieved and its train taken on. The return was with a goods to Woking and vans thence to Southampton.

By this date the Southern, like the other major companies was finding engine maintenance increasingly difficult, consequently uncomplicated two-cylinder 4—6—0s with all the motion readily accessible were highly commended by the sorely harassed shed staffs. Indeed, at Nine Elms 'Lord Nelsons' often could not be prepared in time for their booked duties and had to be replaced by 'N15s' or 'King Arthurs'. As a result, when the LNER

The much fancied 'N15' No. 755 *The Red Knight* fitted with Lemaître blastpipe, large diameter prefabricated chimney and Bulleid pattern 21 in. cylinders.

*R. C. Riley*

'N15' No. 755 *The Red Knight* in malachite green at Salisbury on 20th September 1947, showing clearly the vertical smoke deflector plates and Bulleid cabside numerals.
*H. C. Casserley*

sought the loan of ten 4–6–0s in October 1942, the Southern willingly offered 'Lord Nelsons' Nos. 852/3/7-9/61-5. However, when their four-cylinders became known, they were rejected and, after pressure by the Ministry of War Transport, 'N15s' Nos. 739/40/2/4/7-51/4, were substituted. On the LNER they were stationed at Heaton in the North Eastern Area and mainly employed on goods to Edinburgh, Leeds, Starbeck, Hull and Doncaster, duties shared with classes 'B16' and 'K3'. Occasional passenger trains were also worked, including Leeds-Wetherby-Harrogate, Newcastle-Darlington, Leeds-York-Scarborough and Leeds-Hull, while on 18th December 1942 No. 742 *Camelot* was commandeered from a goods at Berwick to replace an ailing 'A3' on the 10.00 a.m. Edinburgh-King's Cross as far as Newcastle. Equally interesting was the appearance of No. 751 *Etarre* and 'D21' class No. 1243 double-heading the evening Newcastle-Liverpool train on several occasions in March 1943.

Although stationed at Heaton, they joined the common pool and were manned by crews from Gateshead, Tweedmouth, York, St. Margarets and elsewhere. Generally they were well received, with Scottish men accepting them most readily because of the traditional Drummond cab layout. Possibly because of this popularity, they were well-maintained and even cleaned, this being in marked contrast with engines loaned by the Great Western and LMS. All were relieved by USA 2–8–0s and returned to the Southern in July 1943, with No. 744 going to Salisbury and the rest to Eastleigh.

For the remainder of 1943, those stationed at Eastleigh were mainly employed on heavy goods duties, but thereafter, with D-Day approaching, the emphasis changed to passenger work, albeit usually troop specials. By the autumn of 1944 with the land fighting moving deeper into the Continent, many travel restrictions were relaxed until at Christmas the volume of non-military Western Section passenger traffic approached that of 1938 and on several occasions intending travellers had to be turned away at Waterloo because sufficient engines and rolling stock could not be found. As a result, various transfers were made before the summer timetable and these gave an allocation of: Nine Elms No. 755; Eastleigh Nos. 736/7/9-43/7-52/4; Salisbury Nos. 744-6; Exmouth Junction Nos. 738/53.

For some months only limited supplies of malachite green were obtainable and use had to be restricted to the Bulleid Pacifics. Consequently it was April 1946, significantly with No. 755 *The Red Knight*, before the wartime black commenced being replaced. Details are:

| | | | | | | | |
|---|---|---|---|---|---|---|---|
| 736 | 7/1947 | 737 | 10/1946 | 738 | 3/1947 | 740 | 8/1946 |
| 741 | 8/1946 | 742 | 8/1946 | 743 | 12/1946 | 745 | 11/1946 |
| 746 | 7/1946 | 748 | 9/1947 | 749 | 3/1947 | 752 | 3/1947 |
| 755 | 4/1946 | | | | | | |

Nos. 739/44/7/50/1/3/4 did not receive heavy repairs in 1946-7 and therefore were not painted malachite green until after Nationalisation.

At this period locomotive coal was also in short supply so the Government instigated a limited conversion to

'N15' No. 752 *Linette* in Maunsell green with black and white lining, Bulleid lettering and cabside numerals at Bournemouth Central between March 1939 and February 1941.                                                                                              *Photomatic*

'N15' No. 748 *Vivien* in malachite green at Eastleigh after conversion to oil firing and fitted with electric lighting.    *C. L. Caddy Collection*

'N15' No. 30753 *Melisande* in malachite green with BR numbers and Gill Sans tender lettering at Bournemouth in 1948.
*C. L. Caddy Collection*

oil-firing intended to save 5,000,000 tons of coal annually. At Eastleigh ten 'N15s' were laid aside pending conversion, but only Nos. 740/5/8/9/52 had been completed before a foreign currency shortage caused the scheme to be abandoned. Details are:

| No. | To Oil-burning | Electric Lighting Fitted | To Coal-burning |
|---|---|---|---|
| 740 | 14/12/1946 | 3/1/1948 | 30/10/1948 |
| 745 | 4/10/1947 | 4/10/1947 | 18/12/1948 |
| 748 | 29/9/1947 | 13/12/1947 | 20/11/1948 |
| 749 | 11/10/1947 | 28/11/1947 | 20/11/1948 |
| 752 | 27/9/1947 | 20/12/1947 | 2/10/1948 |

The Mexican trough system was employed, with the fuel supply carried in a cumbersome welded tank perched precariously in the tender coal space.

No. 740 *Merlin* steamed erratically when first despatched to traffic and when coasting occasionally extinguished the burners, so it was returned to works for blast-pipe and grate modifications. These proved successful and good performances were given daily on the 7.20 a.m. Eastleigh-Waterloo and the 11.30 a.m. return to Bournemouth West. Nos. 745/8/9/52 entered traffic with these modifications and No. 745 with electric headcode and cab lighting. Nos. 740/8/9/52 were similarly equipped in November 1947 to January 1948.

All five were stationed at Eastleigh and worked such services as the 11.30 a.m. Waterloo-Bournemouth West, 5.05 p.m. Bournemouth West-Waterloo, empty carriage stock and vans to Clapham Junction, slows to Salisbury, Portsmouth and Bournemouth, goods to Salisbury and on one occasion the through Birkenhead to Oxford. By mid-September 1948 most were laid aside awaiting reconversion to coal-firing, the last recorded at work being No. 745 *Tintagel* on 2nd October 1948. Before the end of the year all had been returned to traffic with the oil tanks and other

fittings removed, but retaining the electric lighting and tubular tender ladders.

The class entered British Railways stock at Nationalisation, when all were renumbered into the 30,000 series and painted Brunswick green, although prior to this several carried the temporary S-prefix and were painted malachite green. Details are:

S-PREFIX AND MALACHITE GREEN

| No. | S-prefix | To 30,000 series |
|---|---|---|
| S747 | 24/1/1948 | 12/5/1950 |
| S750 | 7/2/1948 | 6/11/1948 |
| S754 | 17/1/1948 | 3/7/1948 |

No. 753 also received the S-prefix, but this was removed and the 30,000 series number applied in Eastleigh Works yard.

BR NUMBER AND MALACHITE GREEN

| | | |
|---|---|---|
| 30738 5/1949 | 30739 2/1949 | 30742 10/1948 |
| 30743 6/1949 | 30744 6/1948 | 30745 6/1949 |
| 30751 6/1948 | 30753 4/1948 | |

Thereafter, commencing with No. 30741 *Joyous Gard* in September 1949, all repaints were Brunswick green. These dates and those for renumbering and the removal of the snifting valves are:

| No. | BR No. | BR Green Livery | Snifting Valves Removed |
|---|---|---|---|
| 736 | 2/1949 | 11/1950 | 11/1950 |
| 737 | 7/1949 | 6/1951 | 1/1948 |
| 738 | 5/1949 | 1/1953 | 5/1949 |
| 739 | 2/1949 | 5/1952 | 2/1949 |
| 740 | 10/1948 | 5/1950 | 5/1950 |
| 741 | 11/1948 | 9/1949 | 3/1948 |
| 742 | 10/1948 | 12/1951 | 10/1948 |
| 743 | 6/1949 | 6/1953 | 6/1949 |

'N15' No. 30738 *King Pellinore* at Poole on 28th August 1952.                                                    *C. L. Caddy Collection*

| No. | BR No. | BR Green Livery | Snifting Valves Removed |
|---|---|---|---|
| 744 | 6/1948 | 4/1951 | 6/1948 |
| 745 | 12/1948 | 8/1951 | 10/1947 |
| 746 | 9/1950 | 9/1950 | 9/1950 |
| 747 | 5/1950 | 5/1950 | 2/1948 |
| 748 | 11/1948 | 9/1950 | 9/1947 |
| 749 | 11/1948 | 11/1951 | 10/1947 |
| 750 | 11/1948 | 1/1950 | 1/1948 |
| 751 | 6/1948 | 4/1951 | 6/1948 |
| 752 | 9/1948 | 11/1950 | 11/1950 |
| 753 | 4/1948 | 9/1950 | 4/1948 |
| 754 | 7/1948 | 4/1950 | 1/1948 |
| 755 | 10/1949 | 10/1949 | 10/1949 |

Nos. 30738/40-3/50/1/4/5 spent much of the 1949-50 winter in store, but by Easter 1950 most had been returned to traffic in preparation for a busy summer, when the allocation was: Nine Elms Nos. 30742/5/7/55; Feltham No. 30738; Eastleigh Nos. 30749/52; Bournemouth Nos. 736/7/40/1/3/6/50/1/4; Salisbury Nos. 30739/44/8/53. On weekdays Feltham's No. 30738 worked the Reading goods, but on Saturdays it had charge of the 7.36 a.m. Waterloo-Salisbury and the 10.49 a.m. return, the latter being the 12-carriage 8.30 a.m. from Exeter, with a 12.47 p.m. Waterloo arrival. Other Saturday workings were: 29th July Nos. 30737/42/7/55 Bournemouth line; Nos. 30740/1/3/ 51/4 through trains to Bradford, Birmingham, Sheffield, Birkenhead and Newcastle; No. 30739/53 Waterloo-Basingstoke semi-fasts; Nos. 30738/9/44/5/8 Waterloo-Salisbury. Nos. 30744/7 are also worthy of note for the former

worked the 11-carriage 11.25 a.m. Exeter-Waterloo with a loss of only 7 minutes, while No. 30747 did equally well with the 12-carriage 11.35 a.m. Waterloo-Sidmouth Junction (for Exmouth).

During the 1950-1 winter there were few transfers, but before the summer service the allocation was adjusted to bring together consecutively numbered engines, details being: Bournemouth Nos. 30736-43; Feltham No. 30744; Basingstoke No. 30745; Eastleigh Nos. 30746-9; Nine Elms Nos. 30750-5. It is interesting to note that Nine Elms had managed to retain the much fancied No. 30755 *The Red Knight*. On summer Saturdays there were no major duty changes, with No. 30744 *Maid of Astolat* having charge of Feltham's early morning West of England train. This engine was laid aside in store on 24th September 1951, where it remained until transferred to Nine Elms for the Christmas extras. No 'N15' was stationed at Feltham in the following summer, the duty having reverted to Nine Elms and usually entrusted to No. 30752 *Linette*.

A sizeable proportion again entered store in October 1952, therefore when No. 30754 *The Green Knight* failed with fractured frames, it was condemned on 10th February 1953 with a mileage of 1,151,284. Fortunately for the others, the summer Saturday demand remained and in preparation Nos. 30738/41/3/8/53 were given heavy repairs and repaints. Of these No. 30743 *Lyonnesse* was the last Western Section malachite green engine, this having been applied as long ago as June 1949.

The RCTS-promoted Western Section traffic survey of Saturday, 22nd August 1953, gave the following details of 'N15' duties:

'N15' No. 30751, after removal of snifting valves, in malachite green with **BR** number plate and Gill Sans lettering and numerals. *W. Gilburt*

'N15' No. 30737 *King Uther*, with multiple blastpipes and large diameter chimney, in BR lined green livery with first totem, at Eastleigh on 7th July 1951. *Author*

R. C. Riley

'N15' No. 30745 *Tintagel*, with electric lighting, in BR lined green with first totem, at Basingstoke shed on 12th September 1954.

Another view of 'N15' No. 30745 *Tintagel* at Basingstoke on 12th September 1954.

R. C. Riley

| Shed | Allocation | Duties |
|---|---|---|
| Nine Elms | 30744/50-2/5 | No. 30751 7.52 a.m. Waterloo-Bournemouth West and 12.30 p.m. return.<br>No. 30750 10.05 a.m. Waterloo-Bournemouth Central.<br>No. 30752 11.22 a.m. Waterloo-Weymouth and 7.20 p.m. return.<br>No. 30744 2.00 p.m. Ocean Liner special and 5.05 p.m. return.<br>No. 30755 under repair on shed. |
| Basingstoke | 30745/9/53 | No. 30745 6.37 a.m. Basingstoke-Waterloo and then commandeered for 1.05 p.m. Waterloo-Exeter.<br>No. 30753 Basingstoke-Waterloo semi-fasts.<br>No. 30749 up side pilot, not required to assist or replace train engines. |
| Eastleigh | 30747/8 | No. 30747 Channel Island boat.<br>No. 30748 9.02 a.m. Southampton Central-Waterloo and 12.50 p.m. Waterloo-Bournemouth Central. |
| Bournemouth | 30736-43/6* | Nos. 30736-8/46 Through Bradford, Birkenhead, Birmingham and Newcastle.<br>No. 30739 10.00 a.m. Bournemouth Central-Waterloo and 2.34 p.m. return.<br>No. 30740 10.08 a.m. Bournemouth Central-Waterloo.<br>No. 30741 10.20 a.m. Bournemouth West-Waterloo and 3.20 p.m. Weymouth.<br>No. 30742 12.20 p.m. Weymouth-Waterloo.<br>No. 30743 6.35 a.m. Bournemouth Central-Waterloo (slow). |

*On loan from Eastleigh

PERCENTAGE SEEN AT WORK

|               | No. Available | In Traffic No. | % |
|---------------|:---:|:---:|:---:|
| Merchant Navy | 22 | 20 | 91 |
| West Country  | 58 | 45 | 77 |
| Lord Nelson   | 16 | 15 | 94 |
| King Arthur   | 20 | 18 | 90 |
| N15           | 19 | 18 | 95 |

There were no withdrawals in 1954, but 1955 was a year of mixed fortunes, for Nos. 30740/3/6/52 were condemned, Nos. 30738/48/50/1/5 given heavy repairs and no less than fourteen playing an important summer Saturday role. Six more, Nos. 30736/7/41/4/5/7, succumbed in 1956 and were despatched to Brighton Works for breaking up, but after being stripped of sundry minor fittings and detached from its tender, No. 30740 Merlin gained a temporary reprieve so that it could be derailed on the Longmoor Military Railway for a television film. By carefully editing the event, the crash was made to appear most spectacular, although in reality the staging was over-cautious and with little noise or damage Merlin toppled gently into a specially prepared pit. Nos. 30737/53 also gained reprieves for after being laid aside in March 1956 and towed to Brighton Works for breaking up, both were recalled to the Western Section for further service. Before leaving, No. 30753

Melisande made the first recorded appearance of a Urie 'N15' on the Central Section main line, when the Birkenhead through train was worked to and from Redhill on 18th April 1956. The reprieve of No. 30737 King Uther only lasted four months, but No. 30753 Melisande worked an additional 19,034 miles before finally succumbing on 16th March 1957.

By January 1957 the class had dwindled to nine, No. 30738 at Eastleigh, Nos. 30739/42 at Bournemouth, Nos. 30748/50 at Nine Elms and Nos. 30749/51/3/5 at Basingstoke. Several were rusticating in store, so it came as no surprise when Nos. 30739/42/9/51/3/5 were withdrawn and Nos. 30738/48/50 transferred to Basingstoke for the completion of their mileage. No. 30750 Morgan le Fay quickly failed with faulty superheater elements and was sent to Eastleigh Works for breaking up, leaving Nos. 30738/48 to work the Basingstoke-Waterloo semi-fasts and occasional ocean liner specials until the autumn, when the latter was withdrawn. No. 30738 King Pellinore remained active until 8th March 1958, having spent the winter working the Waterloo semi-fasts, van and ballast trains, empty carriage stock and local goods.

In 1959-62 the names carried by the 'N15s' were re-used on British Railways Class 5 4–6–0 Nos. 73080-9 and 73110-9, the plates being replicas of those provided after Grouping, except for omitting the legend 'King Arthur Class'.

'N15' No. 30752 Linette with multiple blastpipes, large diameter chimney and electric lighting at Eastleigh shortly before withdrawal from traffic in 1955.
*Author*

'N15' class No. 30743 *Lyonnesse* at Bournemouth Central on 26th July 1954.          *R. C. Riley*

## ENGINE SUMMARY

| No. | Date | Order No. | Name | Maunsell Superheater | Mileage | Withdrawn |
|---|---|---|---|---|---|---|
| 736 | 8/1918 | N15 | Excalibur | 9/1930 | 1,455,334 | 11/1956 |
| 737 | 10/1918 | " | King Uther | 6/1929 | 1,412,683 | 6/1956 |
| 738 | 12/1918 | " | King Pellinore | 3/1930 | 1,460,218 | 3/1958 |
| 739 | 2/1919 | " | King Leodegrance | 5/1930 | 1,399,989 | 5/1957 |
| 740 | 4/1919 | " | Merlin | 12/1929 | 1,357,971 | 12/1955 |
| 741 | 4/1919 | P15 | Joyous Gard | 2/1929 | 1,346,891 | 2/1956 |
| 742 | 6/1919 | " | Camelot | 8/1930 | 1,386,007 | 2/1957 |
| 743 | 8/1919 | " | Lyonnesse | 6/1930 | 1,301,442 | 10/1955 |
| 744 | 9/1919 | " | Maid of Astolat | 1/1930 | 1,463,292 | 1/1956 |
| 745 | 11/1919 | " | Tintagel | 1/1932 | 1,464,032 | 2/1956 |
| 746 | 6/1922 | L16 | Pendragon | 1/1929 | 1,388,102 | 10/1955 |
| 747 | 7/1922 | " | Elaine | 11/1930 | 1,296,927 | 10/1956 |
| 748 | 8/1922 | " | Vivien | 11/1929 | 1,298,717 | 9/1957 |
| 749 | 9/1922 | " | Iseult | 12/1928 | 1,261,799 | 6/1957 |
| 750 | 10/1922 | " | Morgan le Fay | 2/1930 | 1,298,672 | 7/1957 |
| 751 | 11/1922 | N16 | Etarre | 6/1929 | 1,361,472 | 6/1957 |
| 752 | 12/1922 | " | Linette | 9/1930 | 1,287,576 | 12/1955 |
| 753 | 1/1923 | " | Melisande | 7/1928 | 1,241,374 | 3/1957 |
| 754 | 2/1923 | " | The Green Knight | 1/1930 | 1,151,285 | 2/1953 |
| 755 | 3/1923 | " | The Red Knight | 3/1929 | 1,330,274 | 5/1957 |

All built by Eastleigh Works. Disposal: Nos. 738/9/42/3/6/8-51/3-5 broken up at Eastleigh Works and Nos. 736/7/40/1/4/5/7/52 at Brighton Works. Nos. 736/7/41/52/5 were fitted with Lemaitre blast-pipes and large diameter chimneys in 12/1940, 2/1941, 12/1940, 2/1941 and 2/1940.

Urie 'S15' No. 498 with 5 ft. 7 in. driving wheels, stepped running plates, stove-pipe chimney and 5,000 gallon double bogie tender. *L & GRP, cty. David & Charles*

'S15' No. 498 in photographic grey livery.

*Author's Collection*

# 'S15' Class

The third and final Urie 4−6−0 class, the versatile and powerful 'S15' goods, was designed in conjunction with the express passenger 'N15s' and therefore, apart from the smaller coupled wheels and cylinders, was similar in construction and appearance. Altogether twenty 'S15s' were built by Eastleigh Works in 1920-1, details being:

| Nos. | Ordered | Order No. | To Traffic | Cost |
|---|---|---|---|---|
| 497-501 | 27/1/1916 | S15 | February-June 1920 | £8,405 |
| 502-6 | 29/3/1917 | A16 | July-October 1920 | £9,565 |
| 507-11 | 29/3/1917 | C16 | November 1920-January 1921 | £9,845 |
| 512-5, 496 | 10/10/1918 | E16 | February-May 1921 | £10,230 |

The five 'E16' series were the most expensive engines constructed by the South Western, later orders benefiting by substantially lower material and labour costs. The dimensions were as follows:

| | |
|---|---|
| Cylinders (outside) | 21″ x 28″ |
| Bogie wheels | 3′ 7″ |
| Coupled wheels | 5′ 7″ |
| Wheelbase | 7′ 6″ + 5′ 4½″ + 6′ 3″ + 7′ 6″ = 26′ 7½″ |

| | | |
|---|---|---|
| Boiler | N15 class | |
| Weights in working order: | | |
| | LSWR | Southern (1930) |
| Bogie | 20T 7C | 20T 0C |
| Leading coupled wheels | 18T 14C | 19T 16C |
| Centre coupled wheels | 20T 0C | 19T 19C |
| Trailing coupled wheels | 18T 18C | 20T 1C |
| Engine total | 77T 19C | 79T 16C |
| Tender | 57T 13C | 57T 16C |
| Engine & Tender | 135T 12C | 137T 12C |

In addition to the smaller coupled wheels, the class also differed from the 'N15s' by having 21 inch cylinders, a 10½ in. shorter wheelbase, stepped running plates, a 4½ in. lower boiler pitch, more conspicuous balance weights and a taller stove-pipe chimney. The boiler was fully interchangeable with the 'N15s' and the post-Grouping 'H15s', while the tender was of the standard Urie 5,000 gallon double bogie pattern. Reputedly No. 497 entered traffic in passenger livery, but goods green was applied to the remainder of the class.

After only twelve days in traffic, just sufficient for running-in, No. 515 was returned to Eastleigh Works to be

'S15s' Nos. 508 and 507 as built in goods green livery.

*Author's Collection*

'S15' No. 515 at Eastleigh after conversion to oil firing.                    *Author's Collection*

converted to oil-firing using the Scarab system. The cost of conversion was:

| | |
|---|---|
| 1 main and 2 pilot burners | £136 10s 0d |
| Control valves | £142  5s 0d |
| Piping, clips etc. | £ 13 16s 0d |
| Tender tank (1,400 gallon) | £ 84 18s 0d |
| Labour and Drawing Office | £123 11s 0d |
| Total | £501  0s 0d |

No. 515 ran trials in Eastleigh Works yard on 30th June 1921 and re-entered traffic two days later. At first local passenger and goods services were worked, but on 9th July it was noted in charge of the afternoon Southampton Docks-Salisbury goods. Later, several days were spent working vans and empty coaching stock to Clapham Junction and returning on the ten carriage 11.30 a.m. Waterloo-Bournemouth West. A report submitted by Urie in October 1921 gave the following details of the fuel consumption for the week ending 11th September:

| No. | Fuel Consumption (Train Mile) | | | Cost per |
|---|---|---|---|---|
| | Oil | Coal | Total | Mile |
| 510 | — | 47.7 lb | 47.7 lb | 9.1d |
| 515 | 18.1 lb | 11.2 lb | 29.3 lb | 13.3d |

After working 7,483 miles, No. 515 was reconverted to coal-burning on 17th October 1921.

The remainder of the class were run-in by Eastleigh shed, usually on the 6.10 a.m. Bevois Park sidings-Salisbury and the 11.20 a.m. Salisbury-Eastleigh goods, before being allocated to: Nine Elms Nos. 497-506; Salisbury No. 496; Strawberry Hill No. 507-14 (later also No. 515). At once the following heavy goods duties were allotted the class:

| Nine Elms: | Down | 12.10 a.m. | Nine Elms yard-Eastleigh |
|---|---|---|---|
| | | 12.30 a.m. | Feltham-Salisbury |
| | | 12.55 a.m. | Nine Elms yard-Southampton docks |
| | | 1.45 a.m. | Feltham-Eastleigh |
| | | 2.45 a.m. | Nine Elms yard-Eastleigh |
| | | 7.15 p.m. | Nine Elms yard-Southampton docks |
| | | 8.40 p.m. | Nine Elms yard-Exmouth Junction |
| | | 10.45 p.m. | Nine Elms yard-Salisbury |
| | | 11.15 p.m. | Nine Elms yard-Dorchester |
| | Up | 1.25 p.m. | Southampton docks-Feltham |
| | | 6.17 p.m. | Southampton docks-Nine Elms yard |
| | | 7.20 p.m. | Salisbury-Nine Elms yard (loco coal) |
| | | 7.55 p.m. | Dorchester-Nine Elms yard |
| | | 8.30 p.m. | Exmouth Junction-Nine Elms yard (Market goods) |
| | | 9.15 p.m. | Exmouth Junction-Nine Elms yard (Market goods) |
| | | 9.45 p.m. | Eastleigh-Nine Elms yard |
| | | 10.35 p.m. | Southampton docks-Nine Elms yard (Meat & vegetables) |
| Strawberry Hill: | Down | 5.35 a.m. | Feltham-Southampton docks |
| | | 9.40 a.m. | Feltham-Southampton docks |
| | | 1.40 p.m. | Feltham-Southampton docks |
| | | 10.15 p.m. | Feltham-Southampton docks |
| | Up | 3.10 p.m. | Bevois Park sidings-Feltham |
| | | 2.35 p.m. | Eastleigh-Feltham |
| | | 3.57 p.m. | Southampton docks-Feltham (Citrus fruit) |
| | | 10.05 p.m. | Bevois Park sidings-Feltham |

There were also four return workings to Willesden and one return working to Reading. Salisbury: Two return workings to Eastleigh/Southampton docks.

On summer Saturdays the class was regularly rostered for the Bournemouth and Salisbury reliefs, while most Sundays saw several in charge of seaside excursions. In early 1922 Nos. 500/2/3 were transferred to Strawberry Hill, while No. 515 was sent to Salisbury as a replacement for No. 496, which was on loan to Exmouth Junction.

All entered Southern Railway stock at Grouping to be painted lined goods black and given the E-prefix. By chance these dates were also those of the first general repair, details being:

National Railway Museum

'S 15' No. 511 as built.

'S15' No. 506 at Strawberry Hill on 17th March 1923, and No. 509 at Feltham on 27th October 1923.

*H. C. Casserley*

'S15' No. 505 on 20th October 1924 fresh from Eastleigh Works with standard Southern cabside plates and tender numerals (without the E-prefix) below the LSWR lettering.
*Author's Collection*

| No. | Southern Livery | Mileage | No. | Southern Livery | Mileage |
|---|---|---|---|---|---|
| 496 | 5/1924 | 86,174 | 506 | 12/1924 | 93,648 |
| 497 | 9/1924 | 111,039 | 507 | 3/1925 | 108,474 |
| 498 | 9/1924 | 109,447 | 508 | 11/1925 | 126,361 |
| 499 | 1/1925 | 112,632 | 509 | 6/1926 | 134,112 |
| 500 | 10/1924 | 114,071 | 510 | 1/1925 | 108,903 |
| 501 | 5/1925 | 117,437 | 511 | 10/1925 | 115,679 |
| 502 | 6/1925 | 120,149 | 512 | 9/1925 | 121,476 |
| 503 | 11/1924 | 112,335 | 513 | 7/1924 | 92,513 |
| 504 | 11/1925 | 127,643 | 514 | 4/1925 | 113,099 |
| 505 | 5/1926 (a) | 139,762 | 515 | 1/1926 | 104,803 |

(a) No. 505 received minor repairs at Eastleigh Works in October 1924, when standard Southern cabside numerals were fitted and numerals without the E-prefix added to the tender panels below the LSWR lettering.

To assess the merits of the heavy goods classes taken into stock at Grouping, a series of fuel consumption and haulage trials were held between Bevois Park sidings (Southampton) and Woking in March 1924. Details are:

| No. | Class | Type | No. Engines in Class | Coal Burnt per Train Mile | Comparative Repair Costs* | Remarks |
|---|---|---|---|---|---|---|
| A814 | N | 2—6—0 | 15 | 64.7 lb | 100 | 7½ mins average time lost |
| A822 | N1 | 2—6—0† | 1 | 67.1 lb | 108 | 11 ” ” ” ” |
| B350 | K | 2—6—0 | 17 | 66.2 lb | 117 | 18 ” ” ” ” |
| 510 | S15 | 4—6—0 | 20 | 58.8 lb | 109 | No lost time |

* Ashford N class assessed as 100 units
† Three cylinders

The 'S15' gave an excellent, trouble-free performance and was working well within itself, the acceleration was good and braking strong. 'N' class No. A814 gave a reasonable performance, but the other two classes consistently lost time, despite running excessively fast down the banks, with No. B350 on two occasions overrunning signals. As a result of these findings, twenty-five more 'S15s', Nos. 823-47, were ordered for service on all three Sections.

Because of the 1926 General Strike and the prolonged closure of the coal mines, No. 515 was returned to oil-firing on 12th June 1926 and employed working trains of imported coal from Southampton docks to Oxford (Great Western). This coal came from Poland and was intended for railway use, but the quality proved so abysmal that it had to be relegated to power stations in the Midlands. No. 515 was returned to coal-firing on 17th December 1926.

No spare boilers were provided for the 'N15s' or 'S15s' before Grouping, but this was remedied in December 1924, when eight of 'King Arthur' pattern were ordered from the North British Locomotive Company at a cost of £1,450 each. Three were allotted to the Urie classes, details being:

S15 No. 497 (2/1928); N15s Nos. 737 (10/1925), 742 (12/1925)

Being of Maunsell design, No. 497's new boiler differed by having a 200 lb working pressure, Ross pop safety valves, rim-locking smokebox door, Maunsell superheater and snifting valves. At one time or another all carried a 'King Arthur' boiler.

After general repairs in July 1927, No. 506 was sent to Exmouth Junction as a temporary replacement for newly built Maunsell 'S15' No. 827, which had developed a boiler fault while being run in. On its arrival at Exmouth Junction in mid-September 1927, No. 506 was returned to Feltham.

On summer Saturdays the demand remained for relief passenger service, with Feltham loaning engines as necessary to Nine Elms, Eastleigh and Bournemouth. Generally they were restricted to the more easily timed trains, but if this was not possible their surprisingly good turn of speed made them worthy substitutes for the 'N15s' and 'King Arthurs'. Indeed, many crews preferred them to the 'H15s'. Like the other Urie 4—6—0s, hot boxes proved troublesome when first built, but the problem had been overcome by 1925-6.

'S 15' No. 501 in the Maunsell lined goods black livery with E-prefix.

'S15' No. 513 at Waterloo on 6th August 1927 in Maunsell black livery with E-prefix. *H. G. W. Household*

Possibly because of this regular passenger usage, it was decided to paint the class green in October 1928. Around the same period smoke deflectors were fitted, the E-prefix discarded and Maunsell superheaters substituted for the Eastleigh pattern, details being:

| No. | Green Livery | Maunsell Superheater | Smoke Deflectors | E-prefix Discarded |
|---|---|---|---|---|
| 496 | 7/1930 | 9/1927 | 7/1930 | 2/1933 |
| 497 | 11/1929 | 2/1928 | 11/1929 | 8/1932 |
| 498 | 2/1930 | 2/1930 | 2/1930 | 8/1932 |
| 499 | 6/1931 | 6/1931 | 6/1931 | 1/1934 |
| 500 | 10/1930 | 10/1930 | 10/1930 | 3/1933 |
| 501 | 12/1928 | 8/1931 | 12/1929 | 8/1931 |
| 502 | 1/1930 | 1/1930 | 1/1930 | 7/1932 |
| 503 | 5/1931 | 5/1931 | 5/1931 | 3/1934 |
| 504 | 2/1929 | 2/1929 | 4/1930 | 3/1932 |
| 505 | 9/1929 | 12/1931 | 12/1931 | 12/1931 |
| 506 | 2/1930 | 2/1930 | 7/1932 | 7/1932 |
| 507 | 1/1932 | 1/1932 | 1/1932 | 1/1932 |
| 508 | 4/1932 | 8/1929 | 4/1932 | 4/1932 |
| 509 | 4/1929 | 4/1929 | 7/1932 | 7/1932 |
| 510 | 2/1931 | 2/1931 | 2/1931 | 10/1933 |
| 511 | 11/1930 | 11/1930 | 11/1930 | 9/1933 |
| 512 | 10/1928 | 8/1931 | 8/1931 | 8/1931 |
| 513 | 3/1931 | 5/1930 | 3/1931 | 9/1932 |
| 514 | 4/1934 | 5/1931 | 5/1931 | 4/1934 |
| 515 | 11/1928 | 9/1931 | 11/1928 | 7/1931 |

No. 514 was repainted black on 22nd September 1928, a few days before the decision to substitute passenger green and consequently retained the lined goods black until the next general repair, 10th February to 17th April 1934.

As capable as the class proved in relief passenger service, the Maunsell 'S15s', by virtue of a more advanced front-end,

were better, and consequently they monopolised these workings between Salisbury and Exeter, a line where the original series seldom appeared in passenger service, a segregation exemplified by the mid-1928 allocation of:

| | Urie Series | Maunsell Series |
|---|---|---|
| Nine Elms | Nos. 498/9, 501-4/15 | — |
| Feltham | Nos. 496/7, 500/5-8/10-4 | Nos. 833-7 |
| Salisbury | — | Nos. 828-32 |
| Eastleigh | No. 509 | — |
| Exmouth Junction | — | Nos. 823-7 |

In mid-1929 No. 508 was loaned for several months to Exmouth Junction to cover Nos. 824-6 away at Eastleigh Works, while No. 504 performed a similar duty from May to August 1930 at Salisbury before being transferred to Feltham. Otherwise, except for Feltham gaining No. 509 in October 1935, the allocation was unchanged until World War 2.

In the mid-1930s the other three major companies saw steam as their primary source of motive power for the forseeable future and consequently invested heavily in modern engines and rolling stock. The Southern, however, considered steam obsolescent and channelled most of the available funds towards electrification, a policy which, of necessity, in the interim left the Traffic Department woefully short of large passenger engines on summer Saturdays and led to seven redundant, yet relatively modern ex-LB & SCR 4—6—4 tanks, Nos. 2327-33, being rebuilt as 4—6—0s in 1934-6 for service on the Western Section. Possibly the intention was to reduce reliance on the Urie 'S15' as stand-in express engines for the rebuilds' tenders were obtained from Nos. 504-10, where the loss was made

Two views of 'S15' No. 507 in Maunsell green livery, fitted with 'King Arthur' boiler, capuchonless stove-pipe chimney, and smoke deflectors. In the top view it is paired with a Urie 5,000 gallon double bogie tender, and in the bottom view with a Drummond 'water-cart' tender fitted in August 1935.

*Photomatic and Lens of Sutton*

'S15' No. 504 with 'King Arthur' boiler, capuchonless stove-pipe chimney, smoke deflectors and Drummond 'water-cart' tender at Bedhampton on a Waterloo to Portsmouth excursion on 1st June 1937. *H. E. Simmons*

good by transferring Drummond 4,000 gallon tenders from 'C8' class Nos. 290-6. Details are:

| No. | Tender from | Date | Urie Tender to |
|-----|-------------|------|----------------|
| 504 | 292 | 3/1936 | 2331 |
| 505 | 296 | 12/1935 | 2328 |
| 506 | 291 | 4/1935 | 2333 |
| 507 | 293 | 8/1935 | 2330 |
| 508 | 294 | 3/1935 | 833 (a) |
| 509 | 290 | 1/1935 | 2327 |
| 510 | 295 | 11/1935 | 2332 |

(a) 'N15X' No. 2327 entered traffic with the 5,000 gallon tender of Maunsell 'S15' No. 833, which in exchange received No. 508's tender.

Unfortunately, like many best made plans of mice and men, the scheme floundered when the main line performance of the 'N15Xs' failed to meet expectation and they had to be relegated to secondary passenger duties, leaving the Western Section on summer Saturdays to resound again to the roar of 'S15s' in full flight.

When the 'N15' chimney, blastpipe and motion modifications were finalised in 1925, Eastleigh drawing office considered similar attention for Nos. 496-515, but, for some now unknown reason, no action was taken before November 1930, when No. 511 was fitted with a Maunsell pattern blastpipe and a stovepipe chimney without a capuchon. On trial with Southampton docks and West of England goods, the opinion at Feltham differed whether the steaming was improved, therefore No. 510 was given Maunsell draughting and a 'King Arthur' class chimney in February 1931. Unfortunately, it was to no avail for all agreed that the steaming was atrocious, consequently engines requiring replacement chimneys received capuchonless stovepipes. However, this was only a temporary expedient for on No. 510's return to Eastleigh Works in November-December 1936, it was fitted with an Ashford 'U1' class chimney, which gave a double bonus, since it not only improved the steaming but also the appearance. As a result, Maunsell blastpipe and 'U1' chimneys became standard for the class, details being:

| | | | | | |
|-----|---------|-----|----------|-----|---------|
| 496 | 12/1943 | 497 | 10/1945 | 498 | 8/1941 |
| 499 | 8/1941 | 500 | 12/1940 | 501 | 9/1945 |
| 502 | 2/1947 | 503 | 5/1942 (a) | 504 | 1/1948 |
| 505 | 10/1942 | 506 | 8/1945 | 507 | 8/1940 |
| 508 | 1/1946 | 509 | 7/1946 | 510 | 12/1936 |

511   2/1941        512   6/1946        513  10/1946
514   3/1942 (b)    515  11/1945

(a) The 'U1' chimney fitted to No. 503 in May 1942 was replaced by a 'King Arthur' chimney in March 1945, the 'U1' type being returned in January 1955.

(b) A shortened variation of the 'King Arthur' chimney was carried by No. 514 from May 1931 to July 1936.

The Bulleid livery changes first affected the class in September 1939, details being:

*Maunsell green*, unlined, tender numerals: Nos. 501/4 (September 1939). On both the tender lettering and numerals were painted round, giving a most unusual appearance and a style not repeated by Eastleigh Works.

*Maunsell green*, unlined, Bulleid lettering, cabside numerals: No. 506 (September 1939), Nos. 505/12 (January 1940), 498 (April 1940), 502 (May 1940), 507 (August 1940), 513 (October 1940), Nos. 497, 511 (February 1941).

*Malachite green*, unlined, Bulleid lettering, cabside numerals: Nos. 508 (October 1940), 500 (December 1940).

All later repaints, commencing with No. 509 in April 1941, were plain black.

At first World War 2 had little effect on the class, apart from Nine Elms employing Nos. 498/9, 501-3/15 on the Southampton troop and van specials, but after France fell the heavy main goods service became the major responsibility, with Nos. 498/9, 503 being transferred to Feltham and replaced at Nine Elms by Eastern Section 'King

Arthurs' Nos. 776/81/7. In many respects the Southern was better equipped for the demands of war than the other major companies because the reduced passenger timetable provided a sizeable surplus of versatile 4—6—0s for freight duty. As a result, when the Great Western sought the loan of heavy goods engines in November 1941, Nos. 496-9 could be spared without leaving the Western Section short of motive power. At Feltham they were replaced by 'N15' No. 738 and 'S15s' Nos. 501/2/15 from Nine Elms. On the Great Western the class was Route Colour red and Power Group D, the same as the 'Halls'. At first No. 496 was stationed at Southall and Nos. 497-9 at Old Oak Common for working London area goods, but in February 1942 Nos. 496/8 were transferred to Exeter and appeared on both local passenger and goods services. Before leaving Old Oak, No. 496 received attention to the tubes, while No. 497 was given intermediate repairs at Swindon Works in January 1943 shortly before being transferred to Tyseley. On 18th March 1943 it was recorded on a goods at Chester and on 3rd April 1943 at Wolverhampton. They were replaced by Swindon-built '8F' 2—8—0s, with No. 499 returning to Feltham in March, Nos. 497/8 in May and No. 496 in July 1943.

All heavy repairs were received at Eastleigh Works until September 1942, when the excessive work load led to No. 515 being despatched to Ashford Works. It was routed, subject to a 25 mph speed restriction, via Woking, Guild-

'S15' No. 513 with capuchonless stove-pipe chimney and Bulleid livery of what appears to be unlined black with cabside numerals, passing Winchester on a down goods train.                                                                                                *F. E. Box*

'S15' No. 30505 in unlined black with BR numberplate, Bulleid cabside numbers and Gill Sans tender lettering, at Eastleigh on 16th June 1949, with 'King Arthur' boiler, 'U1' chimney and 'water-cart' tender.

*Author*

'S15' No. 30507 with 'U1' chimney and Urie 5,200 gallon double bogie tender fitted in October 1955. *Photomatic*

ford, Redhill and Tonbridge. On completion of the repairs, it was run-in, probably unofficially and certainly illegally, on the Ashford-Canterbury West-Margate goods. It returned for a second general repair in November 1945, while No. 509 also visited Ashford Works in July 1945.

In February 1944 War Department Riddles 2—8—0s Nos. 7488-97 were loaned to Feltham and immediately took over many main line 'S15' duties, thereby permitting the despatch of Nos. 498, 503/9/10/3/4 to Eastleigh Works for long overdue attention and the repair of others by the shed staff. As a result, when the 2—8—0s were recalled for war service, Feltham's 'S15' link was in excellent fettle.

At Nationalisation all entered British Railways stock to be renumbered into the 30,000 series and painted goods black. Around the same period the smokebox snifting valves were removed and these dates, together with those of renumbering are:

| No. | BR No. | BR Livery | Snifting Valves Removed |
|---|---|---|---|
| 496 | 11/1948 | 11/1948 | 11/1948 |
| 497 | 11/1948 | 11/1948 | 11/1948 |
| 498 | 2/1950 | 2/1950 | 8/1947 |
| 499 | 1/1949 | 1/1949 | 1/1949 |
| 500 | 10/1948 | 10/1948 | 10/1948 |
| 501 | 11/1948 | 11/1948 | 11/1948 |
| 502 | 7/1950 | 7/1950 | 7/1950 |
| 503 | 1/1950 | 1/1950 | 2/1948 |
| 504 | 10/1948 | 10/1948 | 2/1948 |
| 505 | 8/1948 | 1/1950 | 1/1950 |
| 506 | 8/1949 | 8/1949 | 8/1949 |
| 507 | 3/1950 | 3/1950 | 3/1950 |
| 508 | 7/1949 | 7/1949 | 7/1949 |
| 509 | 5/1948 | 5/1948 | 5/1948 |
| 510 | 4/1949 | 4/1949 | 4/1949 |
| 511 | 6/1949 | 6/1949 | 6/1949 |
| 512 | 5/1949 | 5/1949 | 5/1949 |
| 513 | 11/1949 | 11/1949 | 11/1949 |
| 514 | 9/1948 | 9/1948 | 8/1947 |
| 515 | 12/1948 | 12/1948 | 12/1948 |

In April 1948 Nos. 496-8 were replaced at Feltham by 'Q1s' Nos. C9/10/1 and transferred to Nine Elms, but the 0—6—0s did not prove satisfactory substitutes and by December 1949 the three 'S15s' had returned. At Feltham, in addition to the traditional goods duties to Willesden, Neasden, Reading, Salisbury, Fratton, Eastleigh, Southampton and Dorchester, there were summer Saturday Bournemouth reliefs, ocean liner specials and Waterloo-Basingstoke-Salisbury semi-fasts. Occasionally stone ballast specials took the class over the Reading-Redhill line, but the appearance of No. 30515 on the passenger services instead of the usual 'U' class 2—6—0 on 15th January 1953 was most unexpected.

From October 1954 use was made of tenders left spare by withdrawn 'H15s', 'N15s', 'N15Xs' and 'King Arthurs' to replace the 1920 Urie pattern on Nos. 30498/9, 30503 and the Drummond double bogie pattern on Nos. 30504-30510. Details are:

| No. | Tender from | Date | Tender Type |
|---|---|---|---|
| 30498 | 30488 | 10/1954 | Urie 5,200 gallon |
| 30499 | 30835 | 12/1963 | Ashford 4,000 gallon |
| 30503 | 30482 | 1/1955 | Urie 5,200 gallon |
| 30504 | 30487 | 5/1958 | Urie 5,200 gallon |
| 30505 | 30741 | 10/1956 | Urie, 5,000 gallon |
| 30506 | 30745 | 9/1956 | Urie 5,000 gallon |
| 30507 | 30483 | 10/1955 | Urie 5,200 gallon |
| 30508 | 32329 | 11/1956 | Urie 5,000 gallon |
| 30509 | 32328 | 2/1955 | Urie 5,000 gallon |
| 30510 | 30736 | 2/1957 | Urie 5,000 gallon |

'S15' No. 30512 in BR unlined black with first totem. *Author*

Withdrawal commenced with Nos. 30502/4/5 in late 1962, while on 4th February 1963 most of the goods services in the area bounded by Willesden, Reading, Salisbury, Dorchester, Southampton, Fratton and Guildford were transferred to diesel operation. This, of course, removed many traditional 'S15' duties and of those remaining, most were allotted to the Maunsell series, leaving the Uries to cover the Reading goods, occasional interchange workings, local shunting, ECS and substitutions for ailing diesels. Nevertheless, the class still ranged widely, especially No. 30512 which was recorded at Guildford, Eastleigh, Poole and Wilton in May and June 1963. During the final

'S15' No. 30506 on 4th February 1950 with Drummond 'water-cart' tender and BR unlined black livery.                    *Author*

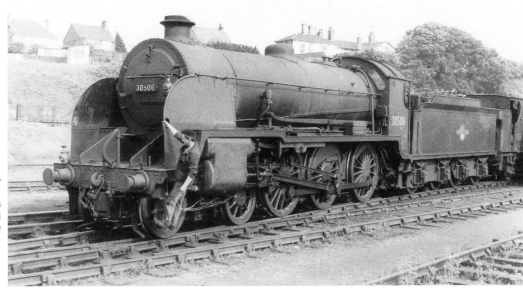

'S15' No. 30506 at Weymouth on 5th June 1963 with Urie 5,000 gallon tender, second totem and AWS battery box on the footplate. *C. L. Caddy*

operational summer Nos. 30506/12 shared the 6.37 a.m. Basingstoke-Waterloo and the 3.54 p.m. return, while the latter played the leading role in the Hayling Island Farewell railtour of 3rd November 1963 and gave a sparkling performance. Probably much to the surprise of the Western Region, No. 30508 was transferred to Exmouth Junction on 14th November 1963, but since it was condemned two days later by that Region, the journey west from Feltham could hardly have taken place. Over the Christmas period No. 30499, 30506/12 were busily engaged working ECS and parcels vans, one of the latter taking No. 30512 to Dorchester on 22nd December, while on 27th December 1963 No. 30499 was noted carriage piloting at Clapham Junction and No. 30512 working ballast hoppers from Woking to Redhill. By this date these three were the only survivors, but not for long because Nos. 30499 and 30506 were condemned on 5th January 1964, leaving No. 30512 to soldier on alone until withdrawn on 4th April 1964 with a mileage of 1,291,002.

At this period Eastleigh was inundated with engines awaiting breaking up, so Nos. 30499, 30506/12 were stored at Feltham and offered for sale. By good fortune they were purchased for £1,040 each by Woodham Brothers of Barry, with No. 30506 being steamed on 18th June 1964 to tow Nos. 30499, 30841/7 to South Wales, but the task proved too strenuous for it failed at Staines and did not complete the journey until the following month. After some months at Feltham, No. 30512 was towed to Eastleigh and thence onwards to Barry, where it was broken up in January 1965 — truly a misfortune because most engines reaching Woodhams yard were left to vegetate and therefore remained available for purchase by preservation groups. As a result, Nos. 30499 and 30506 are with us today, details being:

No. 30499 (boiler No. 755, tender No. 3223 ex-No. 30825):

purchased for £12,650 by the Urie S15 Preservation Group and delivered to the Mid-Hants Railway in November 1983.

No. 30506 (boiler No. 799 ex-No. 30825, tender No. 859): purchased for £6,600 by the Urie S15 Preservation Group and delivered to the Mid-Hants Railway in April 1976. The boiler carried when purchased proved irrepairable, so was replaced by No. 30825s.

## ENGINE SUMMARY

| No. | Date | Order No. | Maunsell Superheater | Mileage | Withdrawn |
|-----|------|-----------|----------------------|---------|-----------|
| 496 | 5/1921 | E16 | 9/1927 | 1,277,029 | 6/1963 |
| 497 | 2/1920 | S15 | 2/1928 | 1,241,163 | 7/1963 |
| 498 | 4/1920 | S15 | 2/1930 | 1,191,462 | 6/1963 |
| 499 | 5/1920 | S15 | 6/1931 | 1,241,024 | 1/1964 |
| 500 | 5/1920 | S15 | 10/1930 | 1,280,116 | 7/1963 |
| 501 | 6/1920 | S15 | 8/1931 | 1,288,684 | 6/1963 |
| 502 | 7/1920 | A16 | 1/1930 | 1,276,916 | 12/1962 |
| 503 | 8/1920 | A16 | 5/1931 | 1,287,774 | 6/1963 |
| 504 | 9/1920 | A16 | 2/1929 | 1,218,025 | 11/1962 |
| 505 | 10/1920 | A16 | 12/1931 | 1,177,241 | 11/1962 |
| 506 | 10/1920 | A16 | 2/1930 | 1,227,897 | 1/1964 |
| 507 | 11/1920 | C16 | 1/1932 | 1,259,244 | 12/1963 |
| 508 | 11/1920 | C16 | 8/1929 | 1,247,861 | 11/1963 |
| 509 | 12/1920 | C16 | 4/1929 | 1,193,769 | 7/1963 |
| 510 | 1/1921 | C16 | 2/1931 | 1,188,192 | 6/1963 |
| 511 | 1/1921 | C16 | 11/1930 | 1,287,933 | 7/1963 |
| 512 | 2/1921 | E16 | 8/1931 | 1,291,002 | 4/1964 |
| 513 | 3/1921 | E16 | 5/1930 | 1,231,659 | 4/1963 |
| 514 | 4/1921 | E16 | 5/1931 | 1,193,977 | 7/1963 |
| 515 | 5/1921 | E16 | 9/1931 | 1,188,683 | 7/1963 |

All built by Eastleigh Works. Disposal: Nos. 496/8, 500-5/8/10/1/3/5 broken up at Eastleigh Works; Nos. 499, 506/12 sold to Woodham Brothers, Nos. 497, 507/9/14 to George Cohen, Kettering. Preserved: Nos. 499, 506 Urie S15 Preservation Group, Mid-Hants Railway.

'G16' class 4—8—0T No. 493, as built with short stove-pipe chimney, at Strawberry Hill on 24th September 1921.

*L & GRP, cty. David & Charles*

'G16' No. 492 in works grey just after completion.          *Author's Collection*

# 'G16' Class

After the turn of the century goods traffic rapidly increased and, although never approaching the volume of the northern coal-carrying companies, nevertheless by 1912 it had overcome the London area marshalling facilities. Appreciating this, the Board authorised the construction of a large gravitation yard and a new motive power depot at Feltham. The land was obtained and the plans finalised by mid-1915, but because of the war little further progress was possible before late 1918, when clearance and drainage of the marshalling yard commenced.

The standard shunter, the 'G6' class 0—6—0 tank, was obviously incapable of heavy hump shunting, therefore in early 1918 drawings were prepared, concurrently with 4—4—2 and 4—6—0 passenger tanks, for a 4—6—0 shunting tank. On being shown the design, the Running Superintendent was critical of the small boiler and 2-ton coal bunker as well as suggesting that eight-coupled wheels would prove advantageous in bad weather. As a result, Urie revised the design and in October 1918 presented the Locomotive Committee with drawings of a large and powerful 4—8—0 tank, of which four were ordered at a cost of £9,535 each from Eastleigh Works. As Nos. 492-5 and classified 'G16', they entered traffic in July-September 1921 and had the following dimensions:

| | |
|---|---|
| Cylinders (outside) | 22″ x 28″ |
| Bogie wheels | 3′ 7″ |
| Coupled wheels | 5′ 1″ |
| Wheelbase | 7′ 6″ + 6′ 6″ + 6′ 0″ + 6′ 0″ + 6′ 0″ = 32′ 0″ |
| Length overall | 42′ 10¼″ |
| Boiler diameter | 4′ 10¾″ |
| Boiler length | 12′ 0″ (Tubeplates 12′ 5″) |
| Firebox length | 8′ 4″ |

| | |
|---|---|
| Heating surfaces: | |
| Small tubes (153 x 1¾″) | 910 sq. ft. |
| Large tubes (21 x 5¼″) | 357 sq. ft. |
| Firebox | 139 sq. ft. |
| Total evaporative | 1,406 sq. ft. |
| Superheater | 231 sq. ft. |
| Total | 1,637 sq. ft. |
| Working pressure | 180 lb |
| Grate area | 27 sq. ft. |
| Tank capacity | 2,000 gallons |
| Bunker capacity | 3½ tons |
| Weights in working order: | |
| Bogie | 22T 4C |
| Leading coupled wheels | 18T 9C |
| Second coupled wheels | 18T 10C |
| Third coupled wheels | 18T 9C |
| Fourth coupled wheels | 17T 10C |
| Total | 95T 2C |

The design was based on the 'S15' goods, although to save weight the boiler was smaller and similar to the 'D15' class 4—4—0s, but to accommodate the second and third coupled axles the firebox was shallower and the grate flatter. Lock-up safety valves were mounted over the firebox and the short stovepipe chimney was provided with a capuchon. Similar boilers were carried by the 'H16' class 4—6—2 goods tanks. The running plate was raised over the cylinders, but dropped behind the expansion link brackets to support the side tanks, which had the leading ends sharply raked to improve cab visibility. Unlike the Urie 4—6—0s, reversing and braking was by steam, both useful assets during lengthy spells of shunting. The cabs were roomy and for steam locomotives relatively comfortable. The combination of small coupled wheels and large cylinders gave the highest tractive effort of any South Western class.

'G16' No. 492 shortly after entering service.

'G16' No. 495 at work in Feltham yard shortly after entering service. *Author's Collection*

'G16' No. 494 at Strawberry Hill on 3rd February 1923. *H. C. Casserley*

'G16' No. 493 at Feltham on 26th July 1924.                                                        *H. C. Casserley*

After being run-in shunting at Eastleigh and working goods to Southampton and Salisbury, No. 492 worked a test train of 45 loaded coal wagons from Bevois Park Sidings to Micheldever on 20th July 1921, with several stops *en route* to discover whether restarting on gradients presented any difficulty. On the following day the same train was worked from Eastleigh to Basingstoke at an average speed of 19.8 mph, while on 22nd July braking tests were held between Brookwood and Barton Mill sidings, when a stop with a train of 55 wagons was made in 1,028 yards. On the return to Eastleigh later in the day, further braking tests were made on the falling gradients after Worting Junction, when the crew had difficulty controlling the train and overran Shawford signals. As this occurred occasionally with the 'S15s', it had been foreseen and the signalman warned to provide a clear path to Eastleigh.

Feltham yard was laid to a seven chain minimum curvature, but in a number of places the curves proved sharper and caused coupling rod and axlebox problems, but these ceased when the bogie play was increased in 1922-3. Another difficulty, which also took time to overcome, was the damage caused when 95 tons of slowly moving steel made contact with rakes of stationary wagons for the smallest error of judgement led to crushed wagon ends and wrecked buffing gear. However, once drivers became accustomed to handling such long and massive

engines within the yard confines, the difficulty ceased and the immense power, sure-footedness and ease of preparation was greatly appreciated.

On the debit side, the grate was overlarge and wasted fuel between shunts, as did the superheater, for every time the regulator was opened, the elements filled with steam, which was immediately dissipated when the regulator was closed, and, since this frequently occurred during shunting, the volume of steam wasted per tour of duty must have been considerable. Additionally, the normal operational speed was too low to raise the firebox temperature sufficiently to provide an appreciable degree of superheat, this being apparent from the water continually dribbling from the cylinder cocks.

In mid-1922 No. 492 was used for a series of trials in the yards at Basingstoke, Bournemouth, Salisbury and Exmouth Junction. No problems arose except at Bournemouth where the layout proved unsuitable for large engines. As a result, four more without superheaters and with bunkers lengthened to carry 5 tons of coal were ordered from Eastleigh Works in September 1922.

As the new marshalling yard opened before the shed, all went new to Strawberry Hill, where they displaced four 'G6s' and three '0395s'.

On weekdays there were three booked duties, two of 17 and 22 hours hump shunting, while the third covered transfer goods to Nine Elms yard, Willesden and Neasden.

This left the fourth engine available to relieve 'H16s' on the Guildford, Reading or Surbiton goods. Occasionally ECS was worked to and from Waterloo until prohibited in October 1922.

All entered Southern Railway stock at Grouping to be painted goods black and receive the E-prefix, details being:

492 9/1924   493 4/1925   494 9/1925   495 5/1924

The September 1922 order was confirmed by Maunsell in July 1923, but construction was postponed to allow work to proceed on the more urgently required 'King Arthurs' Nos. 448-57, while in March 1926 the order was cancelled in favour of the 'Z' class 0—8—0 tanks.

The 'G16s' and 'H16s' retained their own boilers until July 1928, when a spare costing £1,230 was built by Eastleigh Works and fitted to No. 493. Apart from the Maunsell superheater (252 sq ft) and smokebox snifting valves, it was a repeat of the 1921-2 series. The latter were provided with new fireboxes in 1929-32 and Maunsell superheaters in 1929-30, while in later years other changes included the discarding of the E-prefix, the use of unlined black and 15 in numerals, the addition of cab ventilators and the fitting of plain stovepipe chimneys. Details are:

| No. | E-prefix Discarded | Maunsell Superheater | 15 in Numerals | Unlined Black | Cab Ventilators | Plain Stovepipes |
|---|---|---|---|---|---|---|
| 492 | 12/1932 | 5/1930 | 9/1934 | 5/1938 | 5/1938 | 7/1941 |
| 493 | 7/1931 | 7/1928 | 5/1939 | 5/1939 | 5/1939 | 5/1939 |
| 494 | 9/1931 | 12/1929 | 9/1937 | 9/1937 | 2/1941 | 2/1941 |
| 495 | 12/1932 | 3/1930 | 8/1936 | 8/1936 | 1/1938 | 1/1940 |

Similar stovepipe chimneys were fitted to classes 'D15', 'H16', 'L12', 'S11' and 'T14'.

In mid-1939 there were three booked Feltham duties, all hump shunting, although one duty included a return goods to Willesden. However, with the five 'H16s' having to cover a similar number of London area goods duties, the spare 'G16' was frequently called upon to work the Twickenham goods or Durnsford Road power station coal and ash trains. Occasional appearances were also made at Guildford and Reading.

The Bulleid livery changes first affected the class in January 1940, details being:

492 7/1941   493 12/1942   494 2/1941   495 1/1940

All were plain black with bunker numerals.

The rapid expansion of goods traffic from mid-1940 kept the class extremely busy and on 1st September 1940 the number of booked duties was increased to four, these being:

1. Hump shunting at Feltham (18 hours)
2. Hump shunting at Feltham (22 hours)
3. Two return trips to Willesden and one to Neasden
4. Goods to Bracknell, several hours shunting, goods to Reading and vans to Feltham.

All survived hostilities and at Nationalisation entered British Railways stock to be renumbered into the 30,000 series and painted goods black. These dates and those for the removal of the snifting valves are:

'G16' No. 492 in Maunsell goods black livery with 15 inch numerals and E-prefix.

*R. C. Riley Collection*

S. W. Baker

'G16' No. 494, with the plain stove-pipe chimney fitted in 1941 but apparently retaining Maunsell lined goods black livery.

'G16' No. 30493 at Eastleigh on 28th May 1950 in unlined black with BR number and first totem.                                    *W. Gilburt*

| No. | BR No. | BR Livery | Snifting Valves Removed |
|---|---|---|---|
| 492 | 12/1948 | 2/1953 | 12/1947 |
| 493 | 9/1948 | 9/1948 | 9/1948 |
| 494 | 9/1950 (a) | 2/1948 | 2/1948 |
| 495 | 5/1948 | 11/1949 | 5/1948 |

(a) The temporary S-prefix was carried from 21/2/1948 to 1/9/1950.

Apart from the brief appearance of 'Z' class 0—8—0 tank No. A954 in mid-1929, the monopoly of Feltham yard was retained until February 1954, when diesel-electric shunters Nos. 13040-2 arrived from Derby. At once they took over the hump duties, with Nos. 30494/5 being relegated to store and Nos. 30492/3 transferred to the Willesden, Neasden and Guildford goods duties, therefore when the Longmoor Military Railway required the loan of two powerful tanks in October 1954, Nos. 30494/5 could be spared. They worked mainly on the Bordon-Longmoor section and when no longer required were returned to Guildford, from where No. 30495 was despatched to Feltham in November 1954, but, because of a 2—6—0 shortage, No. 30494 was retained until April 1955. Some of the duties worked included passenger services, when tender engines were substituted, although on several occasions it was noted heading empty carriage stock and van trains, while on 17th February 1955 ballast hoppers were worked to Reading.

By mid-1955 only one booked duty remained at Feltham, the Nine Elms yard-Willesden goods, but there were regular substitutions for the 'H16s' and diesel shunters. Because of this all four were retained in stock and in 1955-9 were given heavy repairs and repaints, details being:

30492 12/1956    30493 6/1955    30494 3/1959
30495  4/1958

The fireboxes of Nos. 30492/3 were condemned in January and December 1959, but Nos. 30494/5 remained serviceable, with the transfer of 'H16s' Nos. 30516/7 to Eastleigh for the Fawley oil trains in 1960 ensuring their retention in stock for the time being. Normally they were employed on the Willesden, Neasden and Guildford goods, but on 16th May 1960 No. 30495 was noted at Reading and No. 30494 at Petersfield on 11th November 1961. The former only worked 4,947 miles in 1962, but No. 30494 was kept reasonably busy until replaced by 'Q1' class 0—6—0 No. 33029 in July 1962. Both were condemned at the end of the year.

## ENGINE SUMMARY

| No. | Date | Order No. | Maunsell Superheater | Mileage | Withdrawn |
|---|---|---|---|---|---|
| 492 | 7/1921 | G16 | 5/1930 | 831,931 | 1/1959 |
| 493 | 7/1921 | G16 | 7/1928 | 744,917 | 12/1959 |
| 494 | 8/1921 | G16 | 12/1929 | 823,669 | 11/1962 |
| 495 | 9/1921 | G16 | 3/1930 | 803,687 | 12/1962 |

Built and broken up by Eastleigh Works.

'H16' No. 516 at Strawberry Hill on 3rd February 1923.

H. C. Casserley

'H16' No. 516 when new in Urie lined green livery.
*Author's Collection*

# 'H16' Class

At the April 1912 Locomotive Committee meeting Drummond had the misfortune to be drawn into an acrimonious argument with a director, who recently had travelled on an LB & SCR Eastbourne express headed by a small superheated 4—4—2 tank. He was greatly impressed by the ease with which the heavy, smartly timed train was worked and not unreasonably sought Drummond's professional opinion as to whether similar engines could be employed on the company's secondary main line passenger services. A diplomatic reply drawing attention to the greater South Western distances and the limited water supply of tank engines would probably have ended the discussion, but Drummond's brusque retort drew other Committee members' attention with the result that instructions for the designing of a 4—4—2 tank were issued. However, little progress had been made by Drummond's death, when the scheme was quietly shelved until, prompted by the Locomotive Committee in November 1913, Urie was forced to apply his thoughts to the project and in June 1914 presented drawings of a 4—4—2 tank with 18½ in by 26 in cylinders, 5 ft 7 in coupled wheels, a superheated C8 boiler and 1,500 gallon side tanks. The Locomotive Committee expressed satisfaction with the design, but the 5 ft 7 in coupled wheels, small boiler and inadequate water supply were criticised by the Running Superintendent. As a result, the scheme was abandoned and consideration given to the design of 4—4—2 and 4—6—0 tanks having larger coupled wheels, boilers and water capacity, but because of the war no priority was possible, therefore it was May 1918 before the drawings were completed. Details are:

|  | 4—4—2T | 4—6—0T |
|---|---|---|
| Cylinders (outside) | 19" x 26" | 20½" x 26" |
| Bogie wheels | 3' 7" | 3' 7" |
| Coupled wheels | 6' 7" | 6' 0" |
| Wheelbase | 7' 6" + 8' 3" + 8' 6" + 7' 0" = 31' 3" | 7' 6" + 5' 9" + 7' 0" + 7' 6" = 27' 9" |
| Boiler | L12 class (superheated) | |
| Bunker capacity | 3½ tons | |
| Tank capacity | 1,500 gallons | |

Weights in working order:

|  | 4—4—2T | 4—6—0T |
|---|---|---|
| Bogie | 25T 10C | 24T 0C |
| Leading coupled wheels | 20T 0C | 20T 0C |
| Centre coupled wheels | — — | 20T 0C |
| Trailing coupled wheels | 20T 0C | 20T 0C |
| Radial Truck | 18T 10C | — — |
| Total | 84T 0C | 84T 0C |

Unfortunately, by this date the Running Department no longer required large passenger tanks, but instead powerful tanks capable of working London area interchange goods. This requirement Urie met by stretching the 4—6—0 tank design to accommodate a radial truck, a modified 'D15' class boiler and 2,000 gallons of water, while reducing the coupled wheel diameter to 5 ft 7 in. Five of these 4—6—2 tanks, Nos. 516-20, were ordered from Eastleigh Works at a cost of £9,435 each in October 1918 and entered service at Strawberry Hill between November 1921 and February 1922. The dimensions were as follows:

| Cylinders (outside) | 21" x 28" |
|---|---|
| Bogie wheels | 3' 7" |
| Coupled wheels | 5' 7" |
| Radial truck | 3' 7" |
| Wheelbase | 7' 6" + 6' 0" + 6' 6" + 8' 6" + 8' 0" = 36' 6" |
| Boiler | G16 class |
| Water capacity | 2,000 gallons |
| Coal capacity | 3½ tons |

Weights in working order:

| Bogie | 22T 8C |
|---|---|
| Leading coupled wheels | 19T 16C |

'H16' No. 520 passing Earley station with a Reading-Feltham afternoon freight in 1924.                    *M. W. Earley*

| Centre coupled wheels | 19T 12C |
|---|---|
| Trailing coupled wheels | 19T 12C |
| Radial wheels | 15T 0C |
| Total | 96T 8C |

They were classified 'H16' and had the same boiler, cylinders, motion and bogie as the 'G16' class 4–8–0 tanks, although the cylinders were only bored to 21 in and the coupled wheels were of the same diameter as the 'S15' goods 4–6–0s. The bunker was supported by a radial truck and contained a water tank at the base, thereby permitting the use of lower side tanks without overall loss of capacity as well as removing the need for raking the leading ends to gain good cab visibility. Like the 'G16s', reversing and braking was by steam.

Although large passenger tanks were not currently required by the Running Department, Urie was asked to test the class in semi-fast passenger service; consequently No. 516 worked a series of trial trains between Eastleigh and Bournemouth West in February 1922. In the following month the trials were extended to Bournemouth-Dorchester and Clapham Junction-Basingstoke with trains of four and eight bogie sets. With the heavier loading, the boiler proved inadequate and time was lost, especially between Woking and Basingstoke, where the working pressure seldom exceeded 120 lb, while at 40 to 45 mph the riding was unpleasantly rough. Hot driving boxes also proved troublesome and twice halted the tests. All the running was chimney first, except once from Bournemouth Central to Eastleigh and since this was not repeated, the assumption is that the inspector in charge found the riding unacceptable, although probably not dangerous. Nevertheless, the South Western, Southern and British Railways regularly rostered the class for empty carriage stock duties and the Ascot race specials, albeit chimney first.

Despite being mainly employed working goods services, the class was painted passenger green until World War 2 and because of this became known as the 'Green Tanks', with the 'G16s' becoming the 'Black Tanks', a terminology which remained in force after both classes were painted black.

All entered Southern Railway stock at Grouping to be painted Maunsell green and receive the E-prefix, details being:

'H16' No. 519 at Strawberry Hill.

R. C. Riley Collection

516 7/1926   517 1/1926   518 2/1925   519 8/1925
520 12/1924

The new ownership brought no major duty changes, so the class remained working the London area transfer goods as well as making regular forays to Twickenham, Surbiton, Wimbledon, Woking, Guildford and Reading.

Like the 'G16s', there were few modifications and these mainly concerned the livery, superheater and chimney. Details are:

| No. | Maunsell Superheater | E-prefix Discarded | 15 in. Numerals | Cab Ventilators | Plain Stovepipes |
|---|---|---|---|---|---|
| 516 | 8/1929 | 11/1931 | 5/1935 | 4/1938 | 5/1935 |
| 517 | 5/1929 | 2/1932 | 4/1935 | 7/1938 | 4/1935 |
| 518 | 3/1929 | 6/1932 | 6/1935 | 1/1938 | 6/1935 |
| 519 | 12/1928 | 12/1931 | 2/1935 | 12/1937 | 2/1935 |
| 520 | 12/1929 | 4/1932 | 10/1935 | 10/1938 | 10/1935 |

In May 1939 the five Feltham weekday booked duties were revised to give more economic working, details being:

1. Goods to Nine Elms yard and return, Willesden and return.
2. Goods to Bracknell and Reading, shunting both yards.
3. Goods to Twickenham and return, Durnsford power station and return (this duty to be worked after boiler washout).
4. Goods to Surbiton and Wimbledon, shunting both yards.
5. Return goods to Reading and Willesden (shared with 'S15' class).

If the last mentioned duty was worked by an 'S15', then the spare 'H16' usually substituted for one of the 'G16s'.

The Bulleid livery changes first affected the class in mid-1940, details being:

| No. | Date | Livery |
|---|---|---|
| 516 | 11/1940 | Unlined malachite green (to black 9/1943) |
| 517 | 4/1941 | Unlined black |
| 518 | 12/1941 | Unlined black |
| 519 | 7/1940 | Unlined malachite green (to black 1/1945) |
| 520 | 9/1941 | Unlined black |

All had Bulleid lettering and bunker numerals.

During World War 2 several had lucky escapes in the bombing for No. 520 was on Nine Elms shed when No. 852 *Sir Walter Raleigh* was badly damaged, while No. 519 was narrowly missed by a high explosive bomb at Wimbledon on 17th July 1941. Otherwise, apart from additional Saturday and Sunday duties, hostilities brought few major changes, although No. 520 was noted working a goods through Bournemouth Central on 2nd April 1943 and No. 517 was standing in Salisbury goods yard on 4th September 1944. Both were probably running-in following repair at Eastleigh Works.

All survived hostilities and at Nationalisation entered British Railways stock to be renumbered in the 30,000 series and painted goods black, details being:

516 9/1949   517 7/1948   518 11/1950   519 4/1949
520 11/1948 (a)

These were also the dates when the smokebox snifting valves were removed.

(a) In November 1948 No. 520 was erroneously painted lined black by Eastleigh Works, this being corrected to plain black in October 1951.

'H16' No. 517, with snifting valves and Maunsell lined green livery with E-prefix, at the head of a coal train c.1930.          *Lens of Sutton*

'H16' No. 516 with plain stove-pipe chimney, in Maunsell lined green livery, after removal of the E-prefix.          *R. C. Riley Collection*

'H16' No. 518 on the Chertsey-Weybridge curve with plain stove-pipe chimney, snifting valves and the cab roof ventilator fitted in 1938.

*F. Foote*

C. C. B. Herbert

'H16' No. 30520 in early BR lined black livery at Clapham Junction on 18th June 1949.

All remained working from Feltham, although the five weekday booked duties differed from pre-war, details being:

1. Goods to Nine Elms yard, ECS to and from Waterloo, goods to Willesden and return.
2. ECS to Waterloo from Clapham Junction and Richmond.
3. Goods to Willesden (and return), goods to Reading (and return). Shared with the 'S15' class.
4. Goods to Nine Elms yard, goods to Wimbledon and Surbiton, with lengthy periods of shunting.
5. Goods to Willesden (and return), goods to Wimbledon (and return).

On summer Saturdays there were two booked empty coaching stock duties, which took the class as far afield as Richmond, Hounslow, Chertsey and Walton, while on Sundays vans were worked from Twickenham to Richmond and ECS from there to Waterloo, duties on which a surprisingly good turn of speed was displayed. As a result of No. 520 striking a platform edge at Waterloo in November 1954, use on ECS into London was restricted to chimney first working.

On 25th April 1954 No. 30517 took over the returning RCTS Swindon Works railtour at Reading New Junction and worked it via Ascot and Virginia Water west curve to Chertsey from where, after a brief halt for water, Clapham Junction was reached via Weybridge, Wimbledon and East Putney. The running was excellent with a maximum speed of 55 mph being recorded at Sunningdale and 49½ mph on the main line near Raynes Park, unfortunately at the expense of an overheated left-hand driving box.

In January 1960 No. 30516 was transferred from Feltham to Eastleigh for working the Fawley branch, where marshalling the Esso refinery oil tank trains and their haulage to Totton or Millbrook yards had overcome the capacity of the BR Class 3 2-6-2 tanks. The duty Mondays to Fridays consisted of: piloting the BR Class 3 of the 6.22 a.m. Eastleigh-Fawley passenger train, working the 8.07 a.m. Fawley-Southampton terminus passenger, returning light engine to Eastleigh for a period of carriage piloting before working the 12.50 p.m. empty tankers to Fawley, shunting at Fawley and working tankers to and from Totton or Millbrook until the 7.05 p.m. loaded tanker train to Eastleigh. This strenuous duty was worked continuously until 16th May 1960, when No. 30517 also became available. The spare engine occasionally worked the Alton or Salisbury goods, but more often substituted for the BR

'H16' No. 30516 at Acton Wells Junction with a transfer freight to Feltham on 4th May 1957. *R. C. Riley*

'H16' No. 30518 with first BR totem, at Clapham Junction with a train of parcels stock.    *J. Scrace*

'H16' No. 30518 at Eastleigh on 18th November 1950 in unlined black with first BR totem.    *L. Elsey*

Class 3 on Duty 322, which provided the train engine of the 6.22 a.m. Eastleigh-Fawley and then shunted the refinery sidings until required to pilot the 1.00 p.m. loaded tanker train to Eastleigh. Thereafter it was first choice for marshalling engines on Eastleigh shed.

From Totton and Millbrook block tanker trains were despatched via Salisbury, Westbury and Bristol to Bromford Bridge for distribution in the Birmingham area. Later these services were considerably augmented and to cater for them Nos. 30518/9/20 were also transferred to Eastleigh in January 1961. Unfortunately, by this date all, except No. 30517 which had received heavy repairs in October 1960, were badly run down and failures frequently disrupted the tanker services, so 'W' class 2–6–4 tanks Nos. 31911-3/6/22 were transferred to Eastleigh as replacements in June 1961. No. 30518 had already been returned to Feltham, where Nos. 30516/7/9/20 followed in July 1961. There, only one booked turn remained, covering Clapham Junction-Waterloo ECS and goods to Nine Elms yard, Wimbledon and

Surbiton, consequently most spent lengthy periods in store until withdrawn in November and December 1962. No. 30517 was the last at work, being noted leaving Wimbledon with a goods on Christmas Eve. Previously, it had shared the South Western suburban railtours of 2nd and 16th December 1962 with Beattie well tanks Nos. 30585/7.

## ENGINE SUMMARY

| No. | Date | Order No. | Maunsell Superheater | Mileage | Withdrawn |
|-----|------|-----------|---------------------|---------|-----------|
| 516 | 11/1921 | H16 | 8/1929 | 969,343 | 11/1962 |
| 517 | 11/1921 | H16 | 5/1929 | 893,915 | 12/1962 |
| 518 | 12/1921 | H16 | 3/1929 | 914,639 | 11/1962 |
| 519 | 1/1922 | H16 | 12/1928 | 839,893 | 11/1962 |
| 520 | 2/1922 | H16 | 12/1929 | 886,742 | 11/1962 |

All built by Eastleigh Works. Disposal: Nos. 516/7/9/20 broken up at Eastleigh Works and No. 518 sold to George Cohen Ltd., Kettering.

# Railway Operating Division 2-8-0s

Few engines could be constructed by Eastleigh Works during World War 1 and this, together with the War Department's requisitioning of fifty Adams 0–6–0s, left the South Western extremely short of goods motive power in 1918. Therefore the offer on loan of seventeen Railway Operating Division 2–8–0s in September 1919 was gratefully accepted.

These powerful mineral engines had been developed from the Great Central Railway 8K class for service in France with the Royal Engineers (Railway Operating Division). The first orders were placed in February 1917, with 325 engines being built for war service and a further 196 after the Armistice to provide employment while industry changed from producing munitions and other articles of war to the requirements of peace.

Known as the RODs, the South Western allocation consisted of:

| Date of Delivery | ROD Nos. | Total | Maker |
|------------------|----------|-------|-------|
| 4/11/1919 to 11/11/1919 | 2069-72, 2119-24 | 10 | North British Locomotive Company (Works Nos. 22160-4, 22209-14) |
| 23/1/1920 to 30/1/1920 | 1733/8-42/5 | 7 | Robert Stephenson & Co. (Works Nos. 3760/5-9/72) |

All had been built in 1919 and placed in store on completing their acceptance trials. Nevertheless, their condition on delivery was deplorable for most had been laid aside with undrained boilers, the grates, ashpans and smokeboxes choked with ash, inoperative injectors and damaged coupled wheel boxes. Consequently, it was 14th February

1920 before all were in service, when the allocation became: Strawberry Hill Nos. 2069-72, 2119-24; Eastleigh Nos. 1733/40/2/5; Salisbury Nos. 1738/9/41. Because of their weight and long coupled wheelbase, they were restricted to the following goods duties:

*Strawberry Hill*
2.05 a.m. Feltham-Salisbury, 7.20 p.m. Salisbury-Nine Elms (loco coal); 4.30 a.m. Brentford-Eastleigh, 2.00 p.m. Southampton docks-Nine Elms; 9.40 a.m. Feltham-Eastleigh, 5.40 p.m. Bevois Park sidings-Feltham; 3.10 p.m. Feltham-Eastleigh, 2.50 a.m. Bevois Park sidings-Brentford; 7.35 p.m. Nine Elms-Southampton docks, 6.55 a.m. Eastleigh-Feltham; 10. p.m. Brentford-Eastleigh, 5.40 a.m. Eastleigh-Nine Elms.

*Salisbury*
4.00 p.m. Salisbury-Barton Mills sidings, 11.30 p.m. Basingstoke-Salisbury; 5.33 p.m. Salisbury-Bevois Park sidings, 9.30 p.m. Southampton docks-Salisbury.

*Eastleigh*
6.10 a.m. Bevois Park sidings-Salisbury, 11.20 a.m. Salisbury-Eastleigh; 8.55 a.m. Eastleigh-Salisbury, shunting east yard, 2.00 a.m. (next day) Salisbury-Eastleigh.

The Urie 'S15' class 4–6–0s commenced entering traffic in February 1920 and with their availability the services of the RODs could be dispensed with and by mid-year all were in store or transferred away. Details of disposal are:

Nos. 1739/41 to Great Western Railway March 1920.
Nos. 1738, 2121 to London & North Western Railway June 1920.
Nos. 1733/40/2/5, 2069/71/2, 2120/2/4 to storage at Stratton, Swindon.
Nos. 2070, 2119/23 to storage at Beachley, Chepstow.

The first improved 'N15' No. 453, rebuilt from a Drummond 4—6—0 and retaining the high pitched cab, smokebox door and 'water-cart' tender. This engine was completed at Eastleigh in February 1925 and named *King Arthur*.

R. Randell Collection

# THE MAUNSELL CLASSES

No. 448 *Sir Tristram* in works grey.                    *R. Randell Collection*

# 'King Arthur' Class

In World War 1 Maunsell was seconded by the South Eastern & Chatham Railway to the Railway Executive Committee and was responsible for designing a series of standard passenger and goods classes for service throughout the country. As a result of this involvement, most of the preliminary design work was undertaken by Ashford Drawing Office under the supervision of J. Clayton, the chief draughtsman. G. J. Churchward was also concerned with the project and periodically visited Ashford to monitor progress, therefore it is not surprising that Clayton and Maunsell became aware of current Great Western practice and employed this to advantage when designing the SE & CR 'N' class 2—6—0s and 'K' class 2—6—4 tanks in 1917. Consequently, when given the task of modernising the Urie 'N15' class 4—6—0s after Grouping, he made further use of these precepts by reducing the cylinder diameter, lengthening the valve travel, raising the boiler pressure and substituting the 'N' class smokebox and superheater. Other changes included outside steam pipes, the 'N' class cab, improved lubrication, revised balancing, ashpans with better air circulation and replacing the stovepipes with lipped chimneys. By September 1924 these modifications had been incorporated in the new drawings.

At Eastleigh Works there was an outstanding order for rebuilding fifteen Drummond four-cylinder 4—6—0s, Nos. 330-4 and 448-57, as two-cylinder 'H15s', but the Western Section did not require as many mixed traffic engines, therefore the reconstruction of Nos. 448-57 was changed to modified 'N15s'. At the same time tenders were sought from private manufacturers for the supply of twenty new

engines of similar design. The offers were considered on 17th December 1924, when that of £7,780 each by the North British Locomotive Company was accepted, with delivery scheduled for 31st July 1925. On 28th January 1925 the order was increased to thirty at the same price.

During the reconstruction of Nos. 448-57 at Eastleigh Works, the General Manager's public relations officer, John Elliot, proposed these engines, those being built by the North British and the Urie 'N15s' should be given names of the characters and places mentioned by the Arthurian legends. It was an inspired suggestion which gained immediate acceptance, with modified engines, except *King Arthur* and *Queen Guinevere*, recalling the Knights of the Round Table, while the Urie series were allotted the names of persons and places associated with them.

Nos. 448-57 were returned to traffic as 'improved' 'N15s' or 'King Arthurs' at a cost of £6,320 each between February and July 1925. The dimensions were as follows:

| | |
|---|---|
| Cylinders (outside) | 20½" x 28" |
| Maximum travel | 6 9/16" |
| Steam lap and lead | 1½" & ¼" |
| Bogie wheels | 3' 7" |
| Coupled wheels | 6' 7" |
| Wheelbase | 7' 6" + 5' 6" + 7' 0" + 7' 6" = 27' 6" |
| Boiler diameter | 5' 1 3/8" to 5' 5¾" |
| Boiler length | 13' 9" (Tubeplates 14' 2") |
| Firebox length | 9' 0" |
| Heating surfaces: | |
|    Small tubes (167 x 2") | 1,252 sq. ft. |
|    Large tubes (24 x 5¼") | 464 sq. ft. |
|    Firebox | 162 sq. ft. |

No. 767 *Sir Valence* as built by the North British Locomotive Company, with 'N' class pattern cab, Ashford smokebox door and Urie 5,000 gallon bogie tender. This was one of the first batch completed in May 1925.
*R. Randell Collection*

Eastleigh-built 'King Arthur' No. 452 *Sir Meliagrance* on a West of England express.
*R. Randell Collection*

| Total evaporative | 1,878 sq. ft. | |
|---|---|---|
| Superheater | 337 sq. ft. | |
| Total | 2,215 sq. ft. | |
| Working pressure | 200 lb | |
| Grate area | 30 sq. ft. | |
| Weights in working order: | *Nos. 448-52* | *Nos. 453-7* |
| Bogie | 20T 19C | 20T 15C |
| Leading coupled wheels | 20T 0C | 19T 16C |
| Centre coupled wheels | 20T 0C | 19T 17C |
| Trailing coupled wheels | 20T 0C | 19T 10C |
| Engine total | 80T 19C | 79T 18C |
| Tender | 49T 3C | 49T 3C |
| Engine & Tender | 130T 2C | 129T 1C |

Of the Drummond 4–6–0s little except the high pitched cabs, smokebox doors and 'water cart' tenders remained, but nevertheless Nos. 448-57 were recorded as rebuilds. The tenders, stripped of the wells and feedwater heating equipment, carried 4,300 gallons of water and 5 tons of coal. No. 449 *Sir Torre*, magnificently painted and coupled to a Urie 5,000 gallon tender, represented the Southern Railway at the 1925 Stockton & Darlington Railway Centenary celebrations. The original allocation was: Exmouth Junction Nos. 448/9; Nine Elms Nos. 450-2; Salisbury Nos. 453-7.

Nos. 763-92, ordered from the North British Locomotive Company, were delivered in May to October 1925 and, although also incorporating the Clayton modifications, they differed from the Eastleigh series by having 'N' class pattern cabs, Ashford smokebox doors and Urie 5,000 gallon double bogie tenders. The weight in working order was also marginally greater, details being:

| Bogie | 21T 3C |
|---|---|
| Leading coupled wheels | 20T 0C |
| Centred coupled wheels | 20T 0C |
| Trailing coupled wheels | 20T 0C |
| Engine total | 81T 3C |
| Tender | 57T 11C |
| Engine & Tender | 138T 14C |

After being run-in on the Western Section, Nos. 763-72 were sent to Battersea for the Continental services and Nos. 783-92 to Bournemouth as replacements for unsuccessful 'H15s' Nos. 478, 521-4 on the Waterloo expresses. Nos. 772-82 remained on the Western Section and at Nine Elms displaced 'N15s' Nos. 737/9/40/7 to Exmouth Junction and No. 754 to Salisbury. Although known officially, like Nos. 448-57, as 'King Arthurs', the men always referred to them as 'Scotchmen'.

Much was expected of the 'Improved N15s' and as far as Nos. 448-57 were concerned, the designer was well satisfied, but Nos. 763-92 proved disappointing, especially those working on the Eastern Section for their performance only marginally bettered the ex-SE & CR 'D1s' and 'E1s'. They were also unreliable, although, with the high standard of maintenance then in force, there were few train failures, but substitution on shed was common. Inevitably these shortcomings became known to the General Manager, who called for a report. This was presented in February 1926 and contained the following details:

BOILERS AND FIREBOXES: All thirty boilers have required some degree of caulking, re-riveting and attention to the tubes. The makers employ pneumatic riveting machines, whereas all Eastleigh riveting is performed manually, which avoids 'rivet mushrooming' and subsequent steam blows beneath the boiler cladding. The firebox staying does not follow specification.

HOT COUPLED WHEEL BOXES: These result from engines being assembled with jack support only at the frame extremities, this permits sagging and leads to poorly fitted boxes. All engines have had to be lifted, the boxes forcibly removed, adjusted as necessary and refitted with overall frame support.

BRICK ARCHES: The camber of Nos. 763-82 varied from specification.

TENDER AXLEBOXES: The materials and dimensions of the boxes fitted to the tenders of Nos. 763-82 varied from specification and caused undesirably high running temperatures.

Nos. 763/4/6/7/9/70/3/5/8/90/2: It will be necessary to call these engines to Eastleigh Works before the end of the year.

'Scotch Arthur' No. 771 *Sir Sagramore* between Bickley and Petts Wood Junctions c.1925.

*R. Randell Collection*

A damning indictment of the country's premier loco-motive building establishment — but, since the management grossly underquoted to gain the order, the profit was only £8 12s 7d per engine, and the probability is that 'corners were cut' to save expense. Nos. 763/5-7/72/83 received replacement boilers in 1927-9 and the remainder general repairs, after which the 'Scotchmen' attained their full potential.

Before the structural failings were known, it had been suggested that the shortcomings were caused by the traditional Eastern Section practice of driving with partially open regulators and long cut-offs. Western Section men almost invariably employed fully open regulators and short cut-offs. On becoming aware of the suggestion, Maunsell instigated a series of trials with engines working similar trains and employing both driving methods. Details are:

'Scotchman' No. 777 *Sir Lamiel* as built. *Lens of Sutton*

| No. | Driving Method | Coal burnt per Train Mile | Water Consumed | Lb of water per lb of Coal |
|---|---|---|---|---|
| Victoria-Dover Marine (6 return journeys) | | | | |
| 768 | Regulator | 59.6 lb | 6,382 gallons | 6.91 |
| 778 | Cut-off | 48.6 lb | 5,192 gallons | 6.84 |
| Waterloo-Salisbury (6 return journeys) | | | | |
| 768 | Regulator | 53.2 lb | 6,224 gallons | 6.99 |
| 778 | Cut-off | 48.3 lb | 5,142 gallons | 6.36 |

Both engines were worked by their regular crews, who were given a period of road familiarisation before commen-

cing the trials. As regards coal and water consumption, the findings were an outright win for the Western Section men and No. 778 *Sir Pelleas*, but the time-keeping of both was exemplorary. As a result of these tests, Eastern Section inspectors began commending the use of fully open regulators and short cut-offs; consequently, by the time the 'Schools' class entered service, this method was practised by most top link drivers.

In 1925-6 twenty-five more 'King Arthurs' were ordered from Eastleigh Works, details being:

Another North British-built 'King Arthur' No. 784 *Sir Nerovens*, with Maunsell livery and E-prefix, leaving Waterloo. *R. Randell Collection*

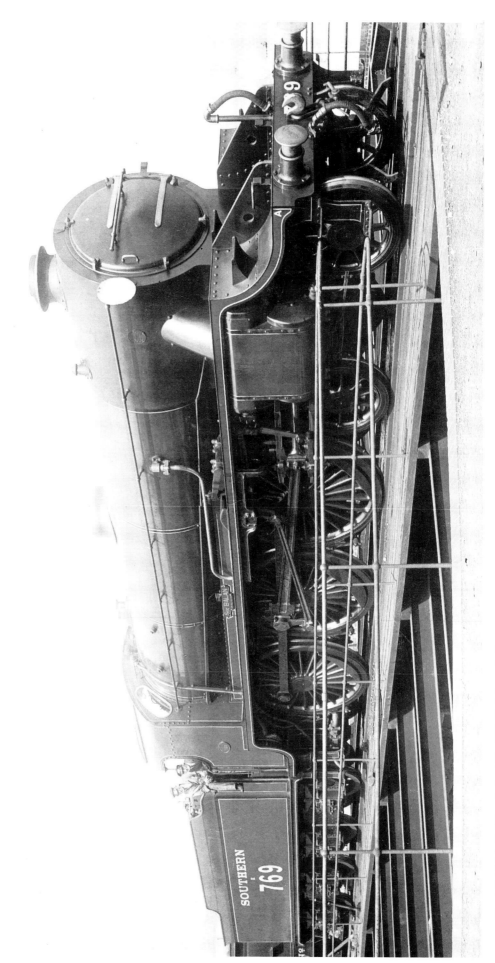

R. Randell Collection

North British built 'King Arthur' No. 769 *Sir Balan* as built.

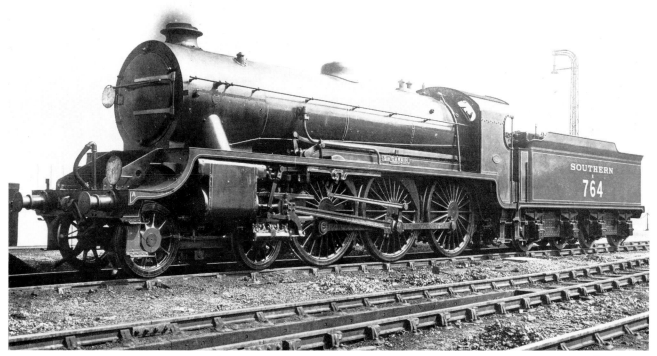

'Scotchmen' No. 766 *Sir Geraint* and No. 764 *Sir Gawain.*                    *Lens of Sutton and R. Randell Collection*

No. 793 *Sir Ontzlake*, the first of the second batch of Eastleigh 'Improved Arthurs', at Stewarts Lane shortly after completion in March 1926. The tender is one of the Ashford 3,500 gallon six-wheel pattern provided for the series.
*Author's Collection*

The small tendered No. 796 *Sir Dodinas le Savage* in original condition.                    *R. Randell Collection*

| Ordered | Nos. | Type of Tender | For Service |
|---------|------|----------------|------------|
| 29/5/1925 | 793-807 | 4,000 gallon | Eastern Section |
| 17/3/1926 | 808-17 | 3,500 gallon | Central Section |

However, only Nos. 793-806 were built, for on 17th June 1926 No. 850 *Lord Nelson* was substituted for No. 807, while on 23rd March 1927 Nos. 808-17 were replaced by 'Lord Nelsons' Nos. 851-60. The intention had been to transfer Eastern Section 'Scotchmen' Nos. 763-72 to Nine Elms and replace them at Battersea with small tendered Nos. 793-807, but, with this no longer possible, it was decided to provide Nos. 763-72 with new 4,000 gallon six-wheel tenders and leave them at Battersea, while diverting Nos. 793-806 to the Central Section. The last mentioned were completed at a cost of £6,300 each between March 1926 and January 1927, the weights in working order being:

| | | |
|---|---|---|
| Bogie | 21T | 5C |
| Leading coupled wheels | 20T | 4C |
| Centre coupled wheels | 20T | 4C |
| Trailing coupled wheels | 20T | 4C |
| Engine total | 81T | 17C |
| Tender | 41T | 5C |
| Engine & Tender | 123T | 2C |

The tenders were of the Ashford 3,500 gallon six-wheel pattern and, because of their higher drawgear, it was necessary to adjust the framing below the cab during construction. This modification was to have unfortunate repercussions for it forbade the temporary substitution of 5,000 gallon Urie tenders on engines loaned to Nine Elms for service on the Western Section.

Nos. 793-5 were delivered to the Central Section in April 1926, but, not having been passed for service between Victoria and Battersea Park, they had to be temporarily stationed at Battersea (Eastern Section) shed and employed on relief Continental expresses, the Victoria-Maidstone East-Ashford semi-fasts, empty coaching stock and van trains. They first reached Brighton on Whit Sunday 1926 at the head of excursions taken over at Battersea yard from the LMS (Midland Division). In July 1926 the Victoria-Battersea Park restriction was removed and Nos. 793-5 could be transferred to Brighton, where later they were joined by Nos. 796-806. Their arrival displaced 'River' tanks Nos. A790-4 to Eastbourne and 'H2s' Nos. B422-6 to Bognor Regis, but, because they were prohibited from working into London Bridge, Brighton had to retain 'Js' Nos. B325/6 and 'Ls' Nos. B327-33 for these services. In addition to the early morning and evening Victoria commuter trains, Nos. 793-806 also worked some of the off-peak Victoria-Eastbourne services. They were well-liked by the men and gave excellent service until electrification. In 1928 Eastleigh commenced a complicated and often bewildering series of tender exchanges involving the 'Lord Nelsons', 'King Arthurs' and Maunsell 'S15s'. To ease explanation, the following tender code will be employed:

F/T:   Urie pattern, double-bogie, 5,000 gallon, flared-top.
F/T/A: Similar to the F/T series, but having auxiliary vacuum cylinders on the tank top.
F/S:   Maunsell pattern, double bogie, 5,000 gallon, flush-sided, auxiliary vacuum cylinders on tank top.
A/4:   Ashford pattern, six-wheeled, 4,000 gallon.

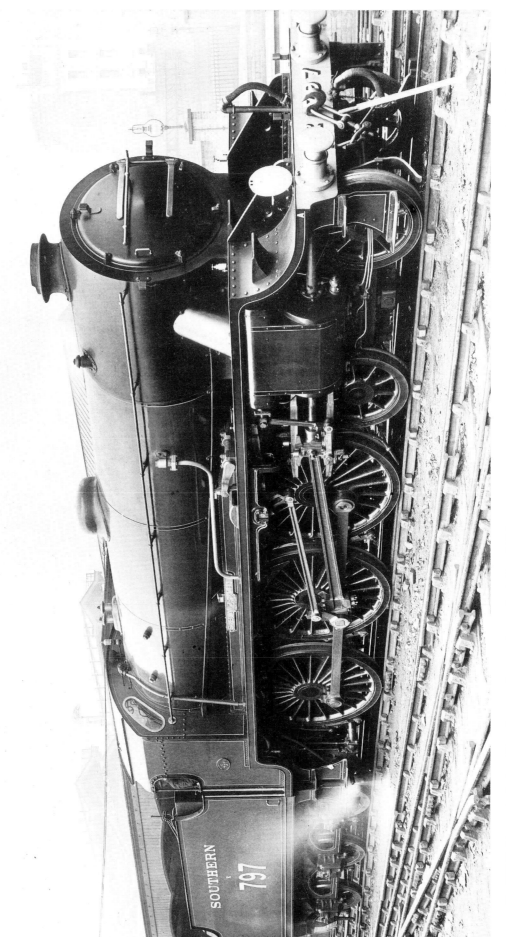

No. 797 *Sir Blamor de Ganis* at Victoria soon after entering service in June 1926.

No. 794 *Sir Ector de Maris* with the distinctive Ashford tender, at Brighton, photographed between 1926 and 1928. *Lens of Sutton*

The first exchanges in 1928-30 concerned 'Lord Nelsons' Nos. 851-60, 'Scotchmen' Nos. 763-72 and Maunsell 'S15s' Nos. 828-37, details being:

| No. | New A/4 Tenders Fitted | Scotchmen's F/T Tender to S15s | S15s F/S Tenders to Lord Nelsons |
|---|---|---|---|
| 763 | 6/1928 | 834 | 854 |
| 764 | 4/1928 | 833 | 851 |
| 765 | 1/1929 | 830 | 860 |
| 766 | 1/1929 | 829 | 859 |
| 767 | 2/1930 (a) | 832 | 853 |
| 768 | 6/1928 | 835 | 855 |
| 769 | (b) | 831 | 852 |
| 770 | 12/1928 | 828 | 858 |
| 771 | 10/1928 | 836 | 856 |
| 772 | 11/1928 | 837 | 857 |

(a) This A/4 tender had seen service on Eastern Section 'Lord Nelson No. 853 from 9/1928 to 2/1930.
(b) During these exchanges No. 769 was transferred from Battersea to the Western Section and consequently did not need an A/4 tender, so its F/T pattern was replaced instead by a new F/S tender. The intended A/4 tender went to Eastern Section 'Lord Nelson' No. 853.

The reason for providing Nos. 763-8/70-2 with A/4 tenders was to avoid having to haul the unnecessarily large F/T pattern on the relatively short distanced Eastern Section journeys. In this context the exchange was successful, but unfortunately when Nine Elms was forced to borrow 'King Arthurs' from Battersea, the A/4 tender lacked capacity for the longer Western Section duties. Consequently a return was made to 5,000 gallon tenders in 1930-7, details being:

| No. | Replacement 5,000 gallon Tender | Date | A/4 Tender to |
|---|---|---|---|
| 763 | F/T ex-833 (a) | 10/1936 | 833 (e) |
| 764 | F/T ex-834 (b) | 11/1936 | 834 |
| 765 | F/T ex-835 (b) | 12/1936 | 835 |
| 766 | F/T ex-836 (b) | 7/1937 | 836 |
| 767 | F/T ex-837 (b) | 6/1937 | 837 |
| 768 | F/S (d) | 1/1930 | 905 (f) |
| 769 | F/S (d) | 12/1929 (c) | – |
| 770 | F/S (d) | 5/1930 | 908 (f) |
| 771 | F/S (d) | 5/1930 | 907 (f) |
| 772 | F/S (d) | 7/1930 | 909 (f) |

(a) Tender originally attached to 'S15' No. 508, later transferred to No. 833.
(b) These tenders were built with 'Scotchmen' Nos. 763/8/71/2.
(c) No. 769 never ran with an A/4 tender.
(d) The F/S tender fitted to Nos. 768-72 were new and later were transferred to 'Lord Nelsons' Nos. 858, 852/9, 853/60.
(e) Nos. 833-7 required A/4 tenders for working on the Central Section where double-bogie tenders were prohibited.
(f) These A/4 tenders, with that from 'Lord Nelson' No. 852, were modified to suit the Tonbridge-Hastings line load gauge and transferred to 'Schools' Nos. 905/8, 907/9, 906.

The final pre-war tender exchanges were comparatively simple for they involved a straight swap between Nos. 768-72 and 'Lord Nelsons' Nos. 858, 852/9, 853/60 in order to provide the latter with latest pattern tenders and thereby giving the class a homogenous appearance. As it happened, this proved a fruitless exercise for as soon as Bulleid became chief mechanical engineer, he provided a non-standard boiler, fitted a variety of large diameter

No. 450 *Sir Kay* with the ineffectual small smoke deflection wings fitted in February 1926.

No. 453 *King Arthur* with the partially effective smoke deflectors fitted in April 1927.                *Lens of Sutton*

No. 772 *Sir Percivale* equipped with the experimental German style shields.                *Lens of Sutton*

chimneys and converted the tenders to self-trimming. Indeed, it was April 1945 before the appearance was again standardised. Details of these tender exchanges are:

| No. | F/T/A Tender from | Date | F/S Tender to |
|-----|------|------|------|
| 768 | 858 (a) | 3/1932 | 853 |
| 769 | 852 | 7/1931 | 852 |
| 770 | 859 | 7/1932 | 858 |
| 771 | 853 | 7/1932 | 859 |
| 772 | 860 | 6/1932 | 860 |

(a) These F/T/A tenders were built with Maunsell 'S15s' Nos. 828/31, 829/32, 830.

At the completion of these exchanges the 'King Arthur' tender position was as follows:

| | | |
|---|---|---|
| F/T | (Urie, double bogie, 5,000 gallon, flared-top) | Nos. 763-7/73-92 |
| F/T/A | (Similar to F/T pattern, except for auxiliary vacuum cylinders) | Nos. 768-72 |
| A/3 | (Ashford, six-wheeled, 3,500 gallon) | Nos. 793-806 |
| Drummond double bogie, 4,300 gallon | | Nos. 448-57 |
| A/4 | (Ashford, six-wheeled, 4,000 gallon) | Not now attached to class |
| F/S | (Maunsell, double bogie, 5,000 gallon, flush-sided) | Not now attached to class |

As the boiler pitch was similar to the Urie 'N15' and the lipped chimney was shorter than their stovepipes, the problem of drifting smoke and steam obscuring the cab look-out was greater. Therefore, in February 1926 small metal wings were fitted behind the chimney of No. 450 *Sir Kay* to combat this danger. On trial between Waterloo and Salisbury, the device proved totally ineffective, so in September 1926 No. 772 *Sir Percivale* was equipped with large German State Railway pattern metal shields on either side of the smokebox. These extended upwards from the platform to 20 in above the boiler centre and, although solving the problem, were so aesthetically disastrous that their general use was unacceptable. As a result No. 453 *King Arthur* was fitted with a pair of smaller and less angular smoke deflectors in April 1927, which did not detract from the appearance, but unfortunately proved only partially effective in calm, damp weather. Therefore, after testing several other devices to no advantage, Maunsell

No. 448 *Sir Tristram* approaching Salisbury on 31st May 1929 complete with the proven deflector plates fitted only three months earlier.
*H. C. Casserley*

No. 806 *Sir Galleron*, the last of the second batch of Eastleigh 'Arthurs', fitted with smoke deflectors but still retaining the E-prefix.
*Lens of Sutton*

'Scotchman' No. 777 *Sir Lamiel* c.1935 with smoke deflectors and retaining the Urie 5,000 gallon double bogie tender.
*R. Randell Collection*

compromised between the deflector plate sizes of Nos. 453 and 772 to obtain the well-known pattern fitted to all the large Urie and Maunsell tender classes. The dates that they were fitted to the 'King Arthurs', together with those for the removal of the E-prefix, are as follows:

| No. | Smoke Deflectors | E-prefix Discarded | No. | Smoke Deflectors | E-prefix Discarded |
|---|---|---|---|---|---|
| 448 | 2/1929 | 5/1933 | 780 | 12/1927 | 7/1932 |
| 449 | 4/1929 | 5/1933 | 781 | 12/1927 | 1/1933 |
| 450 | 12/1927 (a) | 6/1932 | 782 | 12/1927 | 7/1931 |
| 451 | 11/1927 | 5/1932 | 783 | 12/1927 (d) | 2/1932 |
| 452 | 12/1927 | 10/1931 | 784 | 1/1928 | 12/1931 |
| 453 | 4/1927 (b) | 7/1931 | 785 | 2/1928 | 2/1932 |
| 454 | 7/1928 | 8/1932 | 786 | 2/1930 | 4/1932 |
| 455 | 3/1928 | 3/1932 | 787 | 11/1927 | 8/1931 |
| 456 | 3/1928 | 7/1931 | 788 | 12/1927 | 1/1932 |
| 457 | 2/1928 | 8/1932 | 789 | 8/1928 | 1/1932 |
| 763 | 6/1928 | 4/1932 | 790 | 2/1928 | 1/1932 |
| 764 | 4/1928 | 8/1932 | 791 | 1/1928 | 12/1931 |
| 765 | 11/1927 | 4/1933 | 792 | 4/1928 | 1/1932 |
| 766 | 2/1928 | 7/1931 | 793 | 4/1929 | 12/1932 |
| 767 | 4/1928 | 9/1931 | 794 | 5/1928 | 7/1932 |
| 768 | 6/1928 | 3/1932 | 795 | 1/1930 | 1/1932 |
| 769 | 3/1928 | 7/1931 | 796 | 2/1931 | 7/1931 |
| 770 | 3/1928 | 7/1932 | 797 | 1/1929 | 7/1932 |
| 771 | 10/1928 | 4/1932 | 798 | 11/1927 | 2/1933 |
| 772 | 9/1926 (c) | 10/1932 | 799 | 7/1930 | 5/1932 |
| 773 | 12/1927 | 3/1932 | 800 | 11/1927 | 11/1932 |
| 774 | 6/1927 | 7/1931 | 801 | 2/1928 | 10/1932 |
| 775 | 12/1927 | 5/1932 | 802 | 9/1928 | 10/1931 |
| 776 | 12/1927 | 11/1932 | 803 | 3/1928 | 6/1932 |
| 777 | 12/1927 | 6/1932 | 804 | 10/1928 | 6/1932 |
| 778 | 1/1928 | 8/1931 | 805 | 12/1928 | 2/1933 |
| 779 | 4/1927 | 1/1932 | 806 | 4/1928 | 2/1933 |

(a) No. 450 was fitted with small wing plates behind the chimney from 2/1926 to 3/1927.
(b) No. 453 worked with a small version of the standard smoke deflector plates from 4/1927 to 7/1928.

(c) No. 772 carried large German State Railway pattern smoke deflectors from 9/1926 to 10/1932.
(d) No. 783 worked with a shovel-shaped device in front of the chimney from 3/1927 to 12/1927.

Around this period a number of other experimental fittings were carried, including:

Flaman speed recorders: No. 452 10/1927 to 7/1930
No. 782 10/1927 to 12/1930
These did not prove accurate and frequently failed in service.
Bolton Superheater: No. 455 7/1929 to 2/1931
(boiler to No. 454)
No. 454 5/1931 to 8/1932
Tender Tank Gauges: Nos. 791/2 3/1930 to 3/1931

Although 'King Arthur' boilers frequently appeared on the 'N15s', the converse only occurred once, with No. 799 from November 1934 to August 1937. At this period it was stationed at Ramsgate and, despite the lower working pressure, gave spirited performances on the Victoria-Margate expresses.

The practice of allotting new engines in blocks to sheds had administrative advantages, but it also ensured that several engines at a shed became due for heavy repairs at the same time. In the winter months, with fewer passenger duties, this temporary loss of motive power could be overcome by returning stored engines to traffic, but at busy periods it was necessary to borrow from more affluent sheds. Thus Nine Elms regularly had Battersea 'King Arthurs' on loan, while using its own 'N15s' to cover shortages at other Western Section sheds. However, should Battersea require the loan of express engines, it was noticeable that Nine Elms almost invariably supplied 'Lord Nelsons' and retained the 'King Arthur' stud for Western Section service. This borrowing materially reduced the number of permanent transfers; consequently, apart from No. 769 *Sir Balan* sent to Exmouth Junction in mid-1929, the 'King Arthur' distribution remained virtually static until the Central Section electrification of January 1933, when the allocation became: Nine Elms Nos. 452, 773-82;

The rear of Urie 5,000 gallon double bogie tender fitted to 'Scotchman' No. 777 *Sir Lamiel* photographed at Bournemouth on 19th July 1937.

*H. C. Casserley*

'Scotchman' No. 773 *Sir Lavaine* with Urie 5,000 gallon double bogie tender at Bournemouth Central in the mid-1930s.          *Photomatic*

'Scotchman' No. 768 *Sir Balin* at Axminster with Maunsell pattern double bogie 5,000 gallon flush-sided tender fitted new in January 1930. This engine had previously been fitted with the Ashford pattern six-wheeled 4,000 gallon tender in June 1928.     *Collection R. S. Carpenter*

'Scotchman' No. 764 *Sir Gawain* with the Ashford pattern six-wheeled 4,000 gallon tender at Stewarts Lane in 1935.     *Photomatic*

'Improved N15' class No. 450 *Sir Kay* with Drummond 'water-cart' tender, at Waterloo c.1935.

*H. E. Simmons*

'Scotchman' No. 767 *Sir Valence* paired with an Ashford pattern six-wheeled 4,000 gallon tender, leaving Brighton with the 5.35 p.m. up 'Southern Belle' on 30th April 1932. *H. C. Casserley*

Salisbury Nos. 450/1/3-7; Exmouth Junction Nos. 448/9, 769; Bournemouth Nos. 783-92; Battersea Nos. 763-8/70-2/93-6; Ramsgate Nos. 797-806.

At Battersea Nos. 793-6 were usually reserved for the Victoria-Eastbourne services, while Nos. 763-8/70-2 had charge of the Continental and Victoria-Margate expresses. However, should the necessity arise before Nos. 763-7 lost their 4,000 gallon (A/4) tenders, they could work over the Central Section. It was while so employed on 23rd May 1930 that No. 767 *Sir Valence* approached Eastbourne excessively fast with the 5.20 p.m. Victoria and crashed into the buffer stops. As accidents go, with only four serious injuries, it was relatively trivial, but management took the incident extremely seriously for it highlighted the long-standing and pernicious Central Section practice of marshalling heavy and substantially constructed Pullman cars between sets of flimsy non-corridor Billinton wooden carriages. In this instance the train consisted of two 1899 sets, composed of 23 ton carriages, sandwiching two Pullmans together weighing 72 tons. By good fortune the speed of impact was low and much of the momentum was absorbed by *Sir Valence*, but nevertheless the 1st class carriage ahead of the Pullmans was badly crushed. The 'might-have-been' was so horrifying that without waiting for the inspecting officer's report, all Billinton carriages were removed from the Pullman services and replaced by elderly, but substantially constructed, ex-LSWR corridor sets. Henceforth, it was almost unknown for Pullmans to work with non-corridor carriages, except Marsh high-roofed

stock, which presumably was considered capable of holding its own in an emergency.

After a break of twenty years, Pullmans were reintroduced on the Western Section, when No. 780 *Sir Persant* left Waterloo with the inaugural 'Bournemouth Belle' in July 1931, a service which immediately gained popularity, and on Fridays, Saturdays and Sundays was regularly oversubscribed. In 1931-5 the duty on Monday to Friday was shared by Nos. 773-82, with 'Lord Nelsons' having charge on Saturdays and Sundays.

The class regularly visited Dover and in the summer one stabled there overnight, but none were shedded there until May 1934, when Nos. 770/1 were transferred from Battersea, where they were replaced by Nos. 777/8 from Nine Elms. In the autumn Nos. 770/1 returned to Battersea, but they were back the following year and remained working from Dover until mid-1940.

In 1932-3 delays occasionally occurred on the Eastern and Central Sections, when the track circuiting was disrupted by sand deposited on the rails; therefore in March-July 1933 Nos. 763-7/93-6 were fitted with rail-washing equipment. This operated automatically when the forward running sanders were used. 'L12s' Nos. 417/21/6 were similarly equipped in 1933 and 'S15s' Nos. 833-42 in 1936-7. After the outbreak of war the fittings were removed.

No other noteworthy transfers occurred before the Portsmouth electrification of July 1937, when 'Schools' Nos. 924-33 were sent to Bournemouth to replace Nos.

Eastleigh-built No. 804 *Sir Cador of Cornwall* at Salisbury on 20th July 1937.                    *H. C. Casserley*

783/6-92 on the Waterloo services. The latter had performed well and run high mileages between general repairs, but, for speed and fuel economy on these smartly timed and relatively lightly loaded expresses, they were unable to compete with the fine three-cylinder 4—4—0s. The allocation then became: Nine Elms Nos. 772-80; Salisbury Nos. 448-57; Exmouth Junction Nos. 786-92; Bournemouth Nos. 784/5; Battersea Nos. 763-9/81-3/93/4/8/9; Dover Nos. 770/1; Ramsgate Nos. 795-7, 800-6.

Nos. 784/5 were retained by Bournemouth for working the through trains to Oxford, for Waterloo had correctly surmised that the Great Western would refuse to accept the 'Schools' on these services. The Newhaven boat expresses were normally the preserve of the 'H2' class Atlantics, but in the summer months, when loads regularly exceeded their capacity, Battersea avoided piloting by substituting Nos. 793/4/8/9 of the small tender series and therefore acceptable on the Central Section.

In 1934-9 the Southern was fully committed to electrification, but, nevertheless, the existing steam stock was not neglected and maintenance remained as high, if not higher than, the other major companies with the result that very creditable yearly mileages were worked by the principal passenger classes. Details of the 'King Arthurs' are:

*Eastern Section:*

| | | |
|---|---|---|
| Battersea | Nos. 765-9/81-3/93/4/8/9 | 36,100 miles |
| Ramsgate | Nos. 795-7, 800-6 | 35,700 miles |
| Dover | Nos. 770/1 | 35,100 miles |
| Battersea/Ramsgate | Nos. 763/4 | 35,000 miles |

*Western Section:*

| | | |
|---|---|---|
| Nine Elms | Nos. 772-80 | 49,900 miles |
| Salisbury | Nos. 448-57 | 51,600 miles |
| Exmouth Junction | Nos. 786-92 | 44,000 miles |
| Bournemouth | Nos. 784/5 | 57,300 miles |

Such mileages indicate the major express role played by the class before the advent of the Bulleid Pacifics.

In June 1939 the 'King Arthur' and 'N15' booked duties were:

| Shed | Mon-Fri | Saturday |
|---|---|---|
| Nine Elms | 13 | 31 |
| Eastleigh | 4 | 6 (All N15s) |
| Bournemouth | 2 | 2 |
| Salisbury | 14 | 14 (4 N15s) |
| Exmouth Junction | 4 | 9 (1 N15 and 1 S15) |
| Battersea | 8 | 12 |
| Ramsgate | 3 | 4 |
| Dover | 2 | 2 |

**Details of duties:**

*Nine Elms:* The division was approximately 1:2 between the Bournemouth and Salisbury services, with seven of the Saturday duties extended to Exeter. Noteworthy was the number of Saturday duties, far beyond the combined total of 'King Arthurs' and 'N15s', with deficit being made good by upgrading 'H15s' and 'T14s'.

*Eastleigh:* All these duties were 'N15', unless ex-works 'King Arthurs' were to hand. They covered Southampton docks and Bournemouth-Waterloo expresses.

North British-built No. 776 *Sir Galagars*, based at Nine Elms, on the 3.00 p.m. Waterloo to West of England Express at Weybridge.

R. Randell Collection

No. 782 *Sir Brian* at Bromley on 5th March 1939 shortly after receiving a new livery of Maunsell green, black and white lining, Bulleid lettering and cabside numerals the previous month.
*H. C. Casserley*

No. 766 *Sir Geraint* in malachite green and either black and white or black and yellow lining, Bulleid lettering and cabside numerals.
*Lens of Sutton*

No. 777 *Sir Lamiel* leaving Southampton Central in the malachite green livery, Bulleid lettering and cabside numerals applied in January 1947.                                                                                                    *R. Randell Collection*

*Bournemouth:* The through Birkenhead to Oxford and a Waterloo express.

*Salisbury:* All main line duties to Waterloo or Exeter, with the four Saturday 'N15' turns generally being on the lighter and slower trains, although one duty covered the 11.30 a.m. Exeter-Waterloo and another the 98 minute non-stop (10.40 a.m. Waterloo-Exeter) between Salisbury and Exeter.

*Exmouth Junction:* All main line workings to Salisbury during the week and two through trains to Waterloo on Saturdays. The 'N15' duty on Saturdays covered the 8.40 a.m. Exeter-Salisbury slow and the 1.25 p.m. return to Sidmouth Junction.

There was no differentiation between the 'King Arthurs' and 'N15s' in the working diagrams, it being left to the sheds to employ the available motive power to best advantage.

*Battersea:* Continentals and Ramsgate services, approximately in the ratio of 1:2. Any deficiency was made good by 'U1' class 2−6−0s.

*Ramsgate:* To Victoria via Chatham and Charing Cross or Cannon Street via Tonbridge. Any deficiency filled by 'Schools'.

*Dover:* To Charing Cross or Cannon Street via Tonbridge Mondays-Fridays, Continentals on Saturdays.

The Bulleid livery changes first affected the class in late 1938, details being:

Maunsell green, black and white lining, Bulleid lettering, cabside numerals: Nos. 784/5 (December 1938); 451, 764 (January 1939); 776/82/7 (February 1939); 802 (March 1939); 449 (April 1939).

Olive green, yellow and green lining, Bulleid lettering, cabside numerals: Nos. 790 (April 1939); 452/5, 775 (May 1939); 448 (June 1939).

Olive green, yellow and black lining, Bulleid lettering, cabside numerals: Nos. 450, 770/93 (June 1939); 453/7, 800/5 (July 1939); 788 (September 1939); 777, 803 (October 1939); 778/81 (November 1939); 774/86/95/9 (December 1939); 454 (January 1940); 772/80 (February 1940); 773, 806 (May 1940); 456, 768 (June 1940).

Malachite green, black and white lining, Bulleid lettering, cabside numerals: Nos. 766/89 (March 1939).

Malachite green, black and yellow lining, Bulleid lettering, cabside numerals: Nos. 801 (June 1940); 765/9/85 (July 1940); 779/91/8 (August 1940); 452, 792 (September 1940); 449, 783/7 (November 1940); 451, 776 (December 1940); 767/84/9 (January 1941); 450 (February 1941); 453, 790/6 (March 1941); 797 (April 1941); 766 (May 1941); 457 (June 1941); 775 (July 1941); 794 (September 1941); 448, 763/82 (October 1941); 455, 802 (November 1941); 788 (December 1941); 454, 764 (January 1942); 785, 804 (February 1942); 805 (March 1942).

Commencing with No. 456 in April 1942, all later repaints were plain black until January 1946.

From the above lists it will be noted that No. 771 *Sir Sagramore* was the only 'King Arthur' between April 1939 and March 1942 not to be painted either olive or malachite green. Maunsell green livery was retained until replaced by plain black at Ashford Works in September 1942.

In June 1938 authorisation was granted for 16 'Lord Nelsons', 30 'Schools' and 4 'King Arthurs' with Flaman speed recorders at a cost of £70 each. Despite this decision, either by error or design, five 'King Arthurs' were equipped:

451 1/1939     457 8/1938     767 8/1938     779 8/1938
793 6/1939

No. 797 *Sir Blamor de Ganis* in wartime black with Bulleid lettering.                              *Lens of Sutton*

This amenity proved very popular with drivers, but, because of the extra maintenance, the equipment was removed in 1941-2.

At the outbreak of World War 2 there were ten 'Lord Nelsons', Nos. 850/1/3-7/9/61/3, stationed at Battersea for the Folkestone and Dover Continental expresses. These did not immediately cease running, but by late September 1939 there was only a single working in each direction for

non-military traffic; consequently the class was no longer required by the Eastern Section. Therefore, on 8th October 1939, all ten were transferred to Nine Elms and replaced by more versatile 'King Arthurs' Nos. 772-4/7-80/4/5/95, which immediately commenced appearing on the Margate services and main line goods. Other transfers around this period took Nos. 764/7 to Dover, Nos. 798/9 to Ramsgate and Nos. 765/8/9/94/6, 801/6 to Hither Green, the last

Another of the small tender series, No. 795 *Sir Dinadan* in post-war malachite green livery applied in June 1946.    *R. Randell Collection*

mentioned to replace 'S15s' Nos. 838-42 despatched to Feltham. After the fall of France further transfers occurred, many with the intention of removing non-essential engines from the vulnerable coastal sheds. This gave an allocation of: Nine Elms Nos. 775-8/81/2; Salisbury Nos. 448-57; Exmouth Junction Nos. 786-92; Bournemouth No. 774; Battersea Nos. 763-73/80/5/95/9, 801/6; Hither Green Nos. 779/83/4/94/6-8; Ramsgate Nos. 800/2-5.

The 'King Arthurs' were not scheduled for fitting with Lemaître multiple blast pipes and large diameter pre-fabricated chimneys, but No. 792 *Sir Hervis de Revel* had gained such a dismal reputation at Exmouth Junction that Eastleigh was prevailed upon to install this equipment in September 1940. Sadly, it was to no avail, for the erratic steaming and lethargy remained, which led to the Maunsell blast pipe and chimney being refitted in March 1952, when, for no apparent reason, excellent service was given until withdrawal.

Once the threat of invasion had receded, a number of through trains were introduced to enable servicemen and civilians travelling north to south to avoid crossing London. One of the most useful was the Ashford-Newcastle, which was formed of special LNER stock and worked to and from Banbury by the Southern, the Ashford-Reading section by a Ramsgate 'King Arthur' and thence by a Redhill 'U1' class 2—6—0. The route loads were heavy, often 13 or 14 carriages, with the 'U1' frequently requiring a pilot, but the 'King Arthur' had to cope unaided.

Railways are easily seen from the air, especially in daylight when engines discharge steam and smoke. This worried the Ministry of Transport, who asked Eastleigh in November 1940 to conduct a series of trials to discover if the chimney discharge could be concealed without impeding the performance. As a result No. 783 *Sir Gillemere* was equipped as follows:

| November 1940: | Three small diameter stovepipes, exhaust dispersed but performance severely impeded. |
| December 1940: | Two larger diameter stovepipes, exhaust obscured look-out, much less noticeable from air. |
| January 1941: | Plates fitted between the smoke deflectors to give the exhaust extra lift. This they achieved, but all concealment was lost. |
| 15th February 1941: | The trials abandoned and No. 792 returned to traffic with a standard chimney. |

By this date enemy air activity by day was no longer a serious problem, which probably accounted for the sudden loss of interest.

By mid-1941 the heavier loading and additional stops of the Bournemouth services were causing the 'Schools' difficulty, with time being lost regularly by poor acceleration from stops and having to take water *en route*; therefore as a temporary measure Nos. 773/9/81 were transferred to Bournemouth in July 1941 until 'Lord Nelsons' Nos. 850-5 could be released the following year by Nine Elms. Other transfers at this period took Nos. 772/8/93/5 to Eastleigh as replacements for the 'N15s' loaned to the LNER.

As hostilities progressed, so many of the over-harsh pre-war restrictions were eased or cancelled. For the 'King Arthurs' this mainly involved the removal of the Central Section 5,000 gallon restriction, thereby making all the

class, except Nos. 448-57, available for service. As a result, Battersea was able to roster Nos. 763-71/80/5 for Central Section goods duties, although still having to provide one of the small tender 793-806 series should use of the short Three Bridges turntable be necessary. The return of the ten 'N15s' loaned to the LNER in July 1943 led to numerous 'King Arthur' transfers, which ultimately gave the following allocation: Nine Elms Nos. 766-8/70/1/6/80/8; Salisbury Nos. 448-57, 773/4; Exmouth Junction Nos. 775/86/7/9-92; Bournemouth Nos. 772/7/84/5; Battersea Nos. 763-5/9/78/9/81-3/93-6; Ashford Nos. 797-801; Hither Green Nos. 802-6. At Ashford Nos. 797-801 replaced 'H2s' Nos. 2421-6, much to the relief of local crews who had found them heavy on fuel and unsuitable for many Eastern Section secondary passenger duties. At the end of the year 'N1' class 2—6—0s Nos. 1822/76-80 displaced Nos. 802-6 at Hither Green, with the latter going to Ashford, from where Nos. 797-800 moved to Battersea.

No 'King Arthurs' were destroyed by enemy action, but several had lucky escapes, including Nos. 775/6, together with 'N15s' Nos. 751/5, 'N15X' No. 2328, 'Q1' No. C15, 'S15' No. 841 and 'K10' No. 380, at Nine Elms on 20th February 1944, when bomb splinters punctured the tenders and cab sides. Probably the luckiest was No. 806 *Sir Galleron*, which was spectacularly derailed near Newington on 14th July 1944 at the head of a Margate train, when the track ahead was demolished by a 'V2' rocket. It spanned the gap and was not seriously damaged, but the tender took the full weight of the train and was crushed.

After D-day the country sensed that victory was assured and in August 1944 large numbers of women, children and senior citizens converged on Waterloo demanding transport to Bournemouth and the West Country. The initial rush took officials by surprise, but by the second Saturday 'King Arthurs' Nos. 764/9/78/81/3 and several carriage sets had been borrowed from the Eastern Section and most intending passengers were accommodated.

The last V2 fell in Kent on 27th March 1945 and at once the Eastern Section commenced preparations for the changed operating patterns of peace, these included the transfer of Nos. 767-9 to Dover for the Army leave trains. Over the next few months other transfers occurred on both the Western and Eastern Sections, giving an allocation of: Nine Elms Nos. 766/75/7; Salisbury Nos. 448-57, 773/4/84/5; Exmouth Junction Nos. 787/9-92; Bournemouth No. 772; Battersea Nos. 763-5/70/1/6/8-83/6/8/93-9, 800; Ashford Nos. 801-6; Dover Nos. 767-9.

All repaints remained black for some months after VE-day, but as soon as supplies of malachite green became more freely available, it was substituted. Dates of application are:

| | | | | | |
|---|---|---|---|---|---|
| 449 | 11/1947 | 767 | 1/1946 | 776 | 3/1946 |
| 450 | 12/1947 | 768 | 8/1947 | 777 | 1/1947 |
| 451 | 12/1947 | 769 | 5/1947 | 778 | 11/1946 |
| 453 | 9/1947 | 770 | 11/1947 | 779 | 4/1947 |
| 455 | 7/1946 | 771 | 5/1947 | 780 | 3/1947 |
| 456 | 12/1946 | 772 | 7/1947 | 781 | 10/1947 |
| 457 | 1/1947 | 773 | 11/1947 | 783 | 7/1946 (a) |
| 763 | 9/1947 | 774 | 11/1946 | 785 | 6/1947 |
| 766 | 4/1946 | 775 | 10/1946 | 786 | 10/1947 |

No. 30788 *Sir Urre of the Mount* at Bournemouth Central in 1950 or 1951 with spark arrestor and malachite green livery with Gill Sans lettering.
*Author's Collection*

| | | | | | |
|---|---|---|---|---|---|
| 787 | 2/1946 | 795 | 6/1946 | 804 | 5/1947 |
| 788 | 10/1946 | 796 | 12/1946 | 806 | 5/1947 |
| 789 | 3/1946 | 797 | 10/1947 | 765 | 6/1946 (b) |
| 790 | 9/1946 | 798 | 11/1947 | 782 | 4/1947 (b) |
| 792 | 5/1947 | 799 | 1/1947 | 791 | 4/1947 (b) |
| 793 | 4/1946 | 801 | 10/1946 | 800 | 4/1947 (b) |
| 794 | 9/1947 | 802 | 12/1946 | | |

(a) Painted malachite green by Ashford Works, all the remainder by Eastleigh Works. During World War 2 Nos. 764/8/71, 800 also received heavy repairs at Ashford Works.

(b) Temporary shortages of malachite green led to these four leaving Eastleigh Works painted black with green driving wheels.

(c) Nos. 448/52/4, 764/84, 803/5 did not receive general repairs in 1946-7, so remained black.

After the war the quality of coal available for railway use was often poor, which not only adversely affected the steaming, but also increased the risk of lineside fires. These had to be paid for, so in mid-1947 Eastleigh Works commenced a series of trials with large diameter prefabricated chimneys and spark arresters. Details are:

| No. | Date Fitted | Date Removed |
|---|---|---|
| 784 | 6/1947 | 5/1948 |
| 30784 | 2/1949 | 10/1954 |
| 30788 | 12/1949 | 6/1951 |

The steaming was seriously impeded by the chimney fitted to No. 784 in June 1947, so it was removed, modified and refitted in February 1949. This gave acceptable steaming, but failed to control the fire-throwing, therefore a Mark 3 version was prepared and fitted to No. 30788 in December 1949. Success was achieved, but with the quality of coal improving and smokebox spark arresters offering a cheaper and more practical alternative, the trials were abandoned in mid-1951.

All entered British Railways stock at Nationalisation to be renumbered into the 30,000 series and painted Brunswick green. Prior to this, two ran with the temporary S-prefix and thirty were painted malachite green, details being:

S453 from 31/1/1948 to 27/2/1950
S787 from 6/3/1948 to 1/4/1949

### MALACHITE GREEN

| | | | | | |
|---|---|---|---|---|---|
| S453 | 1/1948 | 30767 | 11/1948 | 30789 | 9/1948 |
| S787 | 3/1948 | 30768 | 10/1948 | 30790 | 9/1948 |
| 30448 | 8/1948 | 30772 | 4/1948 | 30791 | 12/1948 |
| 30452 | 5/1948 | 30773 | 6/1949 | 30793 | 10/1948 |
| 30454 | 3/1949 | 30774 | 4/1949 | 30794 | 6/1950 |
| 30455 | 5/1948 | 30777 | 10/1048 | 30795 | 3/1949 |
| 30456 | 10/1948 | 30784 | 5/1948 | 30797 | 1/1949 |
| 30764 | 2/1949 | 30785 | 2/1949 | 30802 | 7/1948 |
| 30765 | 3/1949 | 30786 | 7/1949 | 30803 | 7/1948 |
| 30766 | 1/1949 | 30788 | 10/1948 | 30805 | 10/1948 |

All later repaints were Brunswick green; these dates and those for the removal of the snifting valves are:

| No. | BR No. | BR Green Livery | Snifting Valves Removed |
|---|---|---|---|
| 448 | 8/1948 | 12/1951 | 10/1947 |
| 449 | 9/1949 | 9/1949 | 9/1949 |
| 450 | 9/1949 | 9/1949 | 12/1947 |
| 451 | 7/1948 | 2/1950 | 12/1947 |
| 452 | 5/1948 | 5/1952 | 5/1948 |
| 453 | 2/1950 | 2/1950 | 2/1948 |
| 454 | 3/1949 | 9/1952 | 3/1949 |
| 455 | 5/1948 | 5/1950 | 5/1948 |
| 456 | 10/1948 | 3/1952 | 10/1948 |
| 457 | 8/1949 | 8/1949 | 8/1949 |
| 763 | 6/1950 | 6/1950 | 9/1947 |
| 764 | 2/1949 | 3/1952 | 2/1949 |

No. 30782 *Sir Brian* at Eastleigh on 29th August 1948, apparently still in wartime black but with BR number applied in May 1948.
*W. Gilbert*

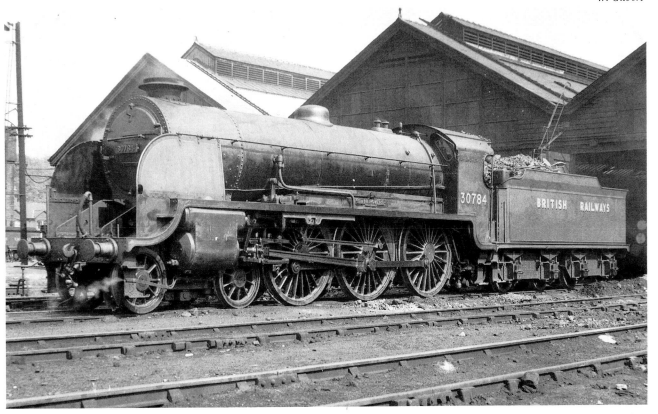

No. 30784 *Sir Nerovens* in malachite green and fitted with spark arrestor, shown here at Eastleigh on 28th June 1949.
*Author*

Small tendered Eastleigh series No. 30805 *Sir Constantine* in malachite green at Hither Green on 10th June 1950.          *W. Gilburt*

No. 30453 *King Arthur*, the first of the class, at Eastleigh on 24th May 1952, three months after receiving the BR green livery and large totem.
                                                                                               *E. W. Fry*

No. 30792 *Sir Hervis de Revel* at Bournemouth Central, in BR green livery, shortly before removal of multiple blastpipes and large diameter prefabricated chimney.  *Author*

| No. | BR No. | BR Green Livery | Snifting Valves Removed |
| --- | --- | --- | --- |
| 765 | 3/1949 | 2/1952 | 3/1949 |
| 766 | 1/1949 | 3/1951 | 11/1947 |
| 767 | 11/1948 | 10/1951 | 11/1947 |
| 768 | 10/1948 | 6/1952 | 10/1948 |
| 769 | 4/1951 | 4/1951 | 4/1951 |
| 770 | 7/1951 | 7/1951 | 11/1947 |
| 771 | 5/1950 | 5/1950 | 5/1950 |
| 772 | 4/1948 | 12/1949 | 7/1947 |
| 773 | 6/1948 | 9/1951 | 11/1947 |
| 774 | 4/1949 | 5/1952 | 4/1949 |
| 775 | 11/1949 | 11/1949 | 11/1949 |
| 776 | 7/1949 | 6/1950 | 12/1947 |
| 777 | 5/1948 | 12/1951 | 10/1948 |
| 778 | 11/1949 | 11/1949 | 11/1949 |
| 779 | 10/1948 | 10/1949 | 10/1948 |
| 780 | 1/1950 | 1/1950 | 1/1950 |
| 781 | 3/1949 | 5/1951 | 10/1947 |
| 782 | 5/1948 | 10/1949 | 10/1949 |
| 783 | 5/1948 | 7/1949 | 5/1948 |
| 784 | 5/1948 | 11/1950 | 5/1948 |
| 785 | 8/1948 | 6/1951 | 2/1949 |
| 786 | 10/1948 | 12/1952 | 10/1947 |
| 787 | 4/1949 | 11/1950 | 3/1948 |
| 788 | 10/1948 | 6/1951 | 10/1948 |
| 789 | 9/1948 | 5/1952 | 9/1948 |
| 790 | 9/1948 | 10/1952 | 9/1948 |
| 791 | 12/1948 | 5/1951 | 12/1948 |
| 792 | 3/1950 | 3/1950 | 3/1950 |
| 793 | 10/1948 | 5/1951 | 10/1948 |
| 794 | 1/1949 | 6/1950 | 9/1947 |
| 795 | 3/1949 | 9/1952 | 3/1949 |
| 796 | 2/1950 | 2/1950 | 2/1950 |
| 797 | 1/1949 | 10/1951 | 10/1947 |
| 798 | 11/1949 | 11/1949 | 11/1947 |

| No. | BR No. | BR Green Livery | Snifting Valves Removed |
| --- | --- | --- | --- |
| 799 | 5/1948 | 6/1950 | 3/1949 |
| 800 | 11/1949 | 11/1949 | 11/1949 |
| 801 | 7/1949 | 3/1951 | 7/1949 |
| 802 | 7/1948 | 1/1951 | 7/1948 |
| 803 | 7/1948 | 12/1951 | 7/1948 |
| 804 | 11/1948 | 2/1950 | 5/1947 |
| 805 | 10/1948 | 12/1951 | 10/1948 |
| 806 | 9/1948 | 11/1950 | 9/1948 |

When well cleaned or recently applied, the Brunswick green suited the class, possibly better than Bulleid malachite, although it did not possess the same excellent weathering quality.

A lengthy series of transfers commenced in January 1951 aimed at gathering engines of the various classes at the running sheds in numerical sequence. By mid-year this gave a 'King Arthur' allocation of: Nine Elms Nos. 30456/7, 30780/1; Salisbury Nos. 30448-55; Bournemouth Nos. 30782/3; Eastleigh Nos. 30784-90; Battersea Nos. 30763-9/77-9/91-5; Bricklayers Arms Nos. 30799, 30800/1; Dover Nos. 30770-6/96-8; Ashford Nos. 30802-5; Hither Green No. 30806. At Dover, Hither Green and Bournemouth these unnecessary transfers caused much ill-feeling, when their well maintained and smartly turned out engines were replaced overnight by the bedraggled residents of the larger sheds. However, this did not deter Hither Green cleaners from setting to work at once on No. 30806 and within 24 hours it was a worthy substitute for the much lamented No. 30800 on the shed's solitary main line passenger turn, the 5.40 p.m. Cannon Street-Ashford. The return was with the 12.50 a.m. goods, which must have been the only freight train in the country always headed by a spotlessly clean engine.

With so many Bulleid Pacifics working on the Western and Eastern Sections, a decline in the demand for 4—6—0s

No. 30779 *Sir Colgrevance*, in BR green livery, leaving Andover Junction with a Waterloo-Salisbury stopping train on 14th May 1955.

*R. C. Riley*

Small-tendered Eastleigh-built No. 30801 *Sir Meliot de Logres* in BR green livery and small totem applied in March 1951. *Photomatic*

on summer Saturdays might have been expected, but in reality the poor Pacific availability ensured that the need remained. This is well illustrated by the 1953 RCTS Traffic Survey, details being:

WESTERN SECTION SATURDAY 22 AUGUST 1953

| Shed | Allocation | Total | Duties |
|---|---|---|---|
| Nine Elms | 30455-7, 30778-81 | 7 | Nos. 30455/6, 30780/1 Bournemouth line Nos. 30778/9 Waterloo-Salisbury No. 30457 8.22 a.m. Waterloo-Exeter and 1.55 p.m. return. |
| Salisbury | 30448-54 | 7 | Nos. 30451/3 Exeter-Waterloo Nos. 30450/2 Salisbury-Waterloo Nos. 30448/54 at Eastleigh Works No. 30449 stopped on shed |
| Eastleigh | 30784-90 | 7 | No. 30785 Bournemouth-Waterloo Nos. 30784/8/90 Channel Island boats Nos. 30787/9 Portsmouth to Western Region No. 30786 stopped on shed |
| Bournemouth | 30782/3 | 2 | No. 30783 through Birmingham No. 30782 at Eastleigh Works |

The class performed well and if not seriously checked by preceding trains, had little difficulty keeping time, but should this occur they took longer to accelerate to full speed than the Pacifics and consequently reduced line capacity. However, of the 20 available, 18 were observed in service, which was a higher proportion than the 'West Countries' for of the 58 available at the four principal sheds only 45 made an appearance.

EASTERN SECTION SATURDAY 1 AUGUST 1953

| Shed | Allocation | Total | Duties |
|---|---|---|---|
| Battersea | 30763-74/91-5 | 17 | Nos. 30764/73/4/91-4 Kent Coast line Nos. 30767/9/70/2 Relief Continentals No. 30795 Through Nottingham No. 30765 worked the 11.26 a.m. Victoria-Ramsgate and returned on the 3.48 p.m. Deal-Charing Cross via Tonbridge Nos. 30763/6/71 at Eastleigh Works |
| Bricklayers Arms | 30799-30801 | 3 | No. 30799 Ferry vans Nos. 30800/1 Charing Cross-Ramsgate |
| Hither Green | 30806 | 1 | No. 30806 8.50 a.m. Charing Cross-Ramsgate |
| Ashford | 30802-5 | 4 | via Tonbridge and 1.42 p.m. Dumpton Park-Victoria Nos. 30802/3 Kent Coast line No. 30804 Charing Cross-New Romney No. 30805 Charing Cross-Deal |
| Dover | 30775-7/96-8 | 6 | Nos. 30775/7 Relief Continentals Nos. 30776/96 Kent Coast line No. 30798 worked the 8.54 a.m. Dover Priory-Charing Cross and 1.57 p.m. Victoria-Deal via Maidstone East No. 30797 ECS Folkestone Junction-Victoria via Tonbridge. |

Again the light Pacifics were conspicuous by their absence, with only 23 of the possible 36 being observed, whereas the 'King Arthur' appearance was virtually total.

There were few duty changes for the following summer, but the delivery of BR Class 5 4-6-0s Nos. 73080-9 to Battersea and BR Class 4 4-6-0s Nos. 75065-9 to Dover in 1955 led to the Eastern Section relinquishing Nos. 30763/70/1 to Basingstoke (replacing withdrawn 'N15Xs'), Nos. 30773/4 to Nine Elms and Nos. 30764/7/91 to Bournemouth.

The withdrawal of classes 'H15', 'N15' and 'N15X' in the mid-1950s left a number of serviceable Urie pattern double bogie tenders spare and advantage was taken of this to replace the Drummond 'water-carts' of Nos. 448-57. Details are:

| No. | Source of Tender | | Date |
|---|---|---|---|
| 30448 | H15 | 30478 | 5/1955 |
| 30449 | N15 | 30743 | 11/1955 |
| 30450 | N15 | 30737 | 10/1956 |
| 30451 | N15X | 32323 | 1/1957 |
| 30452 | KA | 30785 | 6/1957 |
| 30453 | N15 | 30742 | 4/1957 |
| 30454 | N15 | 30755 | 6/1957 |
| 30455 | N15 | 30748 | 12/1957 |
| 30456 | N15 | 30749 | 8/1958 |
| 30457 | H15 | 30490 | 6/1955 |

No. 30770 *Sir Prianius* inside Eastleigh Works on 25th August 1957. This was the last 'King Arthur' to be withdrawn.

R. C. Riley

No. 30763 *Sir Bors de Ganis*, destined to be the last 'Scotchman', at Eastleigh with the second BR totem on 14th June 1958.
*E. W. Fry*

At a later date the Ashford pattern (A/3) tenders of Nos. 30793/5/6/8, 30800/2/3/6 were similarly replaced, details being:-

| No. | Source of Tender | Date |
|---|---|---|
| 30793 | 30776 | 9/1959 |
| 30795 | N15 30738 | 3/1958 |
| 30796 | 30766 | 1/1961 |
| 30798 | 30450 (a) | 10/1960 |
| 30800 | 30454 (a) | 1/1959 |
| 30802 | N15 30750 | 6/1958 |
| 30803 | 30792 | 11/1959 |
| 30806 | N15X 32331 | 8/1958 |

(a) These tenders had seen service with 'N15s' Nos. 30737/55 before being attached to Nos. 30450/5. Nos. 30794/7/9, 30801/4/5 retained 3,500 gallon tenders until withdrawal.

Notwithstanding the delivery of more BR standard 4–6–0s, the class remained fully active until the Kent Coast electrification of June 1959, when all those remaining on the Eastern Section became redundant and were either condemned or transferred to Western Section sheds. These seventeen withdrawals, together with Nos. 30454 and 30766 laid aside the previous year, severely depleted the ranks and by January 1960 the survivors were working from the following sheds: Nine Elms Nos. 30457, 30763/74; Feltham Nos. 30775/7/93/5; Basingstoke Nos. 30456, 30794; Eastleigh Nos. 30768-70/3/88/90/1, 30800/2-4/6; Bournemouth Nos. 30764/5/71/2/81-3; Salisbury Nos. 30448/50/1/3, 30796/8/9. With so many withdrawals the prospects for 1960 were not propitious, but in fact Nos. 30453, 30765/73/7/82/8/95/8 all received heavy repairs and repaints, while on Saturdays throughout the summer Nos. 30457, 30763/73/88, 30800/3/4/6 appeared regularly on the Bournemouth reliefs, Nos. 30451/5, 30765/82/93/9 on the Waterloo-Basingstoke-Salisbury semi-fasts and No. 30783 on the 6.37 a.m. Exeter-Waterloo slow and the 4.03 p.m. Clapham Junction-Yeovil milk tankers. On

several occasions No. 30790 headed the 9.02 a.m. Southampton Central-Waterloo and the 1.40 p.m. ECS to Eastleigh, while on 20th August No. 30804 recalled earlier years by working the ten carriaage 10.56 a.m. Exeter through to Waterloo.

The withdrawal of Nos. 30448/50/6, 30763/9/74/5/91/4 in 1960 led to the transfer of Nos. 30777/93/5 to Basingstoke, Nos. 30771/83 to Salisbury and No. 30764 to Bournemouth, while in January 1961 No. 30451 was the last to receive a general repair. Many of the survivors spent the winter in store and, with further Eastern Section electrification releasing more Pacifics in June 1961, there were fewer calls to main line service on summer Saturdays. The most consistent performer was No. 30798 *Sir Hectimere* which successfully worked the 9.25 a.m. Wimbledon-Weymouth and the 3.50 p.m. return on five occasions.

By the end of 1961 only twelve remained in stock, Nos. 30773/88, 30804 at Eastleigh, Nos. 30451, 30796/8 at Salisbury, Nos. 30781/2 at Bournemouth and Nos. 30865/70/93/5 at Basingstoke. Those at Eastleigh shared the midday Clapham Junction stock train and the 7.25 p.m. goods from Nine Elms yard until withdrawn in February 1962, while Salisbury's Nos. 30451 and 30798 regularly worked up to Waterloo with the 8.46 a.m. and returned with the 2.54 p.m., leaving No. 30796 to cover station piloting and occasional ballast trains. During the summer only No. 30770 *Sir Prianius* appeared regularly on the Bournemouth reliefs, ocean liner specials and Channel Island boats, while after the commencement of the winter timetable, it alone remained in stock working ECS, van trains and local goods until withdrawn on 24th November 1962.

### PRESERVATION

In November 1960 it was decided to preserve a member of the class, therefore when No. 30653 *King Arthur* was withdrawn on 8th July 1961, it was placed in store pending refurbishment. Unfortunately, although it remained basically

No. 30453 *King Arthur* at Nine Elms shed on 6th September 1958 coupled to the Urie double bogie tender which, fitted in April the previous year, would prevent it from being preserved.

*R. C. Riley*

sound, all the Drummond 'water cart' tenders originally coupled to the Eastleigh 'Arthurs' had been broken up, and, since a Urie pattern tender would be inappropriate, it had to be rejected and replaced by North British built No. 777 *Sir Lamiel*. After a lengthy period of store at Fratton, Stratford and Ashford, *Sir Lamiel* was transferred to the Humberside Preservation Group at Hull in June 1978. There the boiler was retubed, several frame fractures welded, the wheels dropped, the boxes remetalled and the tender lifted before steam was raised on 21st February 1982. Later, in Maunsell green livery, it returned to main line service with the Cumbrian Mountain Pullman on 27th March 1982.

## ENGINE SUMMARY

| No. | Name | Date | Order No. | Mileage | Withdrawn |
|-----|------|------|-----------|---------|-----------|
| 448 | Sir Tristram | 5/1925 | C17 | 1,483,140 | 8/1960 |
| 449 | Sir Torre | 6/1925 | " | 1,373,426 | 12/1959 |
| 450 | Sir Kay | 6/1925 | " | 1,478,783 | 9/1960 |
| 451 | Sir Lamorak | 6/1925 | " | 1,579,556 | 6/1962 |
| 452 | Sir Meliagrance | 7/1925 | " | 1,494,011 | 8/1959 |
| 453 | King Arthur | 2/1925 | B17 | 1,606,428 | 7/1961 |
| 454 | Queen Guinevere | 3/1925 | " | 1,421,676 | 10/1958 |
| 455 | Sir Launcelot | 3/1925 | " | 1,475,829 | 4/1959 |
| 456 | Sir Galahad | 4/1925 | " | 1,386,742 | 5/1960 |
| 457 | Sir Bedivere | 4/1925 | " | 1,429,723 | 5/1961 |

All built and broken up by Eastleigh Works.

| No. | Name | Date | | Mileage | Withdrawn |
|-----|------|------|--|---------|-----------|
| 763 | Sir Bors de Ganis | 5/1925 | | 1,050,454 | 10/1960 |
| 764 | Sir Gawain | 5/1925 | | 979,213 | 7/1961 |
| 765 | Sir Gareth | 5/1925 | | 1,116,054 | 9/1962 |
| 766 | Sir Geraint | 5/1925 | | 1,141,019 | 12/1958 |
| 767 | Sir Valence (a) | 5/1925 | | 1,029,937 | 6/1959 |
| 768 | Sir Balin | 5/1925 | | 1,078,112 | 11/1961 |
| 769 | Sir Balan | 6/1925 | | 1,036,794 | 2/1960 |
| 770 | Sir Prianius | 6/1925 | | 1,144,608 | 11/1962 |
| 771 | Sir Sagramore | 6/1925 | | 1,054,549 | 2/1961 |
| 772 | Sir Percivale | 6/1925 | | 1,187,768 | 9/1961 |
| 773 | Sir Lavaine | 7/1925 | | 1,296,365 | 2/1962 |
| 774 | Sir Gaheris | 6/1925 | | 1,121,270 | 1/1960 |
| 775 | Sir Agravaine | 6/1925 | | 1,136,498 | 2/1960 |
| 776 | Sir Galagars | 6/1925 | | 1,094,727 | 1/1959 |
| 777 | Sir Lamiel | 6/1925 | | 1,257,638 | 10/1961 |
| 778 | Sir Pelleas | 7/1925 | | 1,174,925 | 5/1959 |
| 779 | Sir Colgrevance | 7/1925 | | 1,305,864 | 7/1959 |
| 780 | Sir Persant | 7/1925 | | 1,112,973 | 7/1959 |
| 781 | Sir Aglovale | 8/1925 | | 1,184,126 | 5/1962 |
| 782 | Sir Brian | 7/1925 | | 1,197,719 | 9/1962 |
| 783 | Sir Gillemere | 8/1925 | | 1,221,647 | 3/1961 |
| 784 | Sir Nerovens | 8/1925 | | 1,369,983 | 10/1959 |
| 785 | Sir Mador de la Porte | 9/1925 | | 1,314,287 | 10/1959 |
| 786 | Sir Lionel | 9/1925 | | 1,389,822 | 8/1959 |
| 787 | Sir Menadeuke | 9/1925 | | 1,304,180 | 2/1959 |
| 788 | Sir Urre of the Mount (b) | 9/1925 | | 1,423,378 | 2/1962 |
| 789 | Sir Guy | 9/1925 | | 1,383,297 | 12/1959 |
| 790 | Sir Villiars | 9/1925 | | 1,404,162 | 11/1961 |
| 791 | Sir Uwaine | 9/1925 | | 1,353,546 | 5/1960 |
| 792 | Sir Hervis de Revel | 9/1925 | | 1,351,319 | 2/1959 |

All built by the North British Locomotive Company (Works Nos. 23209-28 and 23279-88).
(a) Originally allotted the name *Sir Mordred*.
(b) Originally allotted the name *Sir Beumains*.
Disposal: All broken up at Eastleigh Works, except No. 788 at Ashford Works and No. 777 preserved.

| No. | Name | Date | Order No. | Mileage | Withdrawn |
|-----|------|------|-----------|---------|-----------|
| 793 | Sir Ontzlake | 3/1926 | E121 | 979,964 | 9/1962 |
| 794 | Sir Ector de Maris | 3/1926 | " | 903,663 | 8/1960 |
| 795 | Sir Dinadan | 4/1926 | " | 963,712 | 8/1962 |
| 796 | Sir Dodinas le Savage | 4/1926 | " | 1,061,295 | 3/1962 |
| 797 | Sir Blamor de Ganis | 6/1926 | " | 953,718 | 6/1959 |
| 798 | Sir Hectimere | 6/1926 | " | 1,093,868 | 6/1962 |
| 799 | Sir Ironside | 7/1926 | " | 1,001,005 | 2/1961 |
| 800 | Sir Meleaus de Lile | 9/1926 | " | 960,510 | 9/1961 |
| 801 | Sir Meliot de Logres | 10/1926 | " | 939,617 | 4/1959 |
| 802 | Sir Durnore | 10/1926 | " | 1,096,024 | 7/1961 |
| 803 | Sir Harry le Fise Lake | 11/1926 | " | 989,396 | 9/1961 |
| 804 | Sir Cador of Cornwall | 12/1926 | " | 1,115,634 | 2/1962 |
| 805 | Sir Constantine | 1/1927 | " | 1,019,198 | 11/1959 |
| 806 | Sir Galleron | 1/1927 | " | 1,127,096 | 4/1961 |

All built by Eastleigh Works. Disposal: All broken up at Eastleigh Works, except No. 804 at Ashford Works.

## REPAIR COSTS (PER MILE) 1954-5

| Class | Engine | Boiler | Tender & Shops Overheads | Total |
|-------|--------|--------|--------------------------|-------|
| | d | d | d | d |
| King Arthur | 8.25 | 1.94 | 1.82 | 12.01 |
| N15 | 8.38 | 1.92 | 1.78 | 12.08 |
| Schools | 7.82 | 1.65 | 1.67 | 11.14 |
| Lord Nelson | 8.08 | 1.70 | 1.84 | 11.62 |
| West Country | 9.13 | 2.01 | 1.93 | 13.07 |

## REPAIRS 1950-5

| | General to Intermediate | | Between General Repairs | |
|--|----|----|----|----|
| | Miles | Months | Miles | Months |
| Nos. 448-57 | 86,264 | 20.0 | 120,458 | 39.6 |
| Nos. 763-92 | 82,870 | 23.4 | 109,544 | 45.5 |
| Nos. 793-806 | 72,044 | 26.3 | 107,290 | 45.9 |
| King Arthur (average) | 79,791 | 23.7 | 111,376 | 44.2 |
| Lord Nelson | 85,338 | 19.3 | 138,202 | 36.9 |
| Schools | 79,447 | 23.2 | 148,274 | 43.1 |
| West Country | 73,992 | 18.4 | 206,425 | 47.2 |

## GENERAL REPAIRS AND MILEAGES

| General Repairs | No. 763 Sir Bors de Ganis (New 5/1925) | | No. 770 Sir Prianius (New 6/1925) | |
|--|----|----|----|----|
| | Date | Mileage | Date | Mileage |
| 1st | 8/1927 | 73,884 | 6/1927 | 75,288 |
| 2nd | 6/1928 | 33,682 | 3/1931 | 72,667 |
| 3rd | 2/1931 | 79,143 | 2/1933 | 87,032 |
| 4th | 9/1933 | 89,929 | 10/1934 | 79,835 |
| 5th | 11/1935 | 91,448 | 10/1936 | 86,425 |
| 6th | 6/1938 | 91,172 | 6/1939 | 86,457 |
| 7th | 10/1941 | 78,859 | 1/1943 | 89,882 |
| 8th | 1/1945 | 91,909 | 6/1945 | 107,086 |
| 9th | 9/1947 | 74,532 | 11/1947 | 75,340 |
| 10th | 6/1950 | 70,658 | 7/1951 | 102,629 |
| 11th | 4/1953 | 74,996 | 4/1954 | 63,999 |
| 12th | 6/1958 | 132,147 | 8/1951 | 92,929 |
| To withdrawal | 1/10/1960 | 68,093 | 24/11/1962 | 124,989 |
| Total mileage | | 1,050,454 | | 1,144,608 |
| Average yearly mileage | | 30,013 | | 30,935 |
| Average mileage between general repairs | | 81,863 | | 84,968 |

'S 15' No. 833 as built with straight running plate, Ashford style cab, 'King Arthur' pattern chimney and Urie pattern 5,000 gallon double bogie tender. Finished in goods black, it is shown here shortly after entering service.

*Author's Collection*

# Maunsell 'S15' Class

The main line freight haulage and fuel consumption trials of April and May 1924 conclusively proved that the Urie 'S15' class 4—6—0s were the best Southern Railway heavy goods engines. Therefore, when more engines of this type were required in May 1925, Maunsell had no hesitation in placing an order at Eastleigh Works for ten more of a modified and improved design at a cost of £6,585 each. These also gave excellent, trouble-free service and during the next eight years were followed by fifteen more, to give a final class total of twenty-five, details being:

| Ordered | Nos. | Delivery | Cost |
|---|---|---|---|
| 1/5/1925 | 823-32 | March to November 1927 | £6,585 |
| 17/3/1926 | 833-7 | November 1927 to January 1928 | £6,400 |
| 19/3/1931 | 838-47 | May to December 1936 | £5,430 |

The construction of Nos. 838-47 was postponed twice because of the trade depression and was only commenced in March 1936 with Government financial assistance.

The dimensions were as follows:

| | |
|---|---|
| Cylinders (outside) | 20½″ x 28″ |
| Bogie wheels | 3′ 7″ |
| Coupled wheels | 5′ 7″ |
| Wheelbase | 7′ 6″ + 5′ 4½″ + 6′ 3″ + 7′ 6″ = 26′ 7½″ |
| Boiler | King Arthur class |

| Weights in working order: | Nos. 823-37 | Nos. 838-47 |
|---|---|---|
| Bogie | 20T 14C | 20T 0C |
| Leading coupled wheels | 20T 0C | 19T 11C |
| Centre coupled wheels | 20T 0C | 19T 18C |
| Trailing coupled wheels | 20T 0C | 19T 16C |
| Engine total | 80T 14C | 79T 5C |
| Tender | 57T 11C | 56T 8C |
| Engine & Tender | 138T 5C | 135T 13C |

Just as the Urie 'S15s' had been designed in conjunction with the express passenger 'N15s', so Nos. 823-47 were the heavy goods equivalent of the 'King Arthurs' and therefore incorporated the refinements introduced after grouping by Maunsell. These included 20½ in diameter cylinders, longer valve travel, outside steam pipes, larger port and steam pipe areas, improved draughting, enlarged ashpans and a Maunsell superheater. The boiler pitch was the same as the 'N15s' and 'King Arthurs', while the running plate was straight, the cab modelled on the Ashford 2—6—0s and the chimney of 'King Arthur' pattern. The 5,000 gallon double bogie tenders of Nos. 823-32 were of Urie pattern, with those of Nos. 828-32 having vacuum cylinders behind the coal space on the tank tops, while those built with Nos. 833-47 were partially welded and flush-sided. Nos. 838-47 entered

'S15' No. 825 at Eastleigh in April 1927. Following official photography in fully lined grey livery, the locomotive and tender has been returned to works for finish painting in Maunsell goods black. *Roye England*

'S15' No. 836 at Feltham shortly after completion, in goods black with Maunsell partially welded and flush-sided double bogie tender.

Author's Collection

'S 15' No. 836 passing through Clapham Junction with a passenger train on 9th April 1928. The Maunsell tender was transferred to a 'Lord Nelson' in November 1928 when it was replaced by a Urie pattern 5,000 gallon double bogie example from a 'King Arthur'. *H. C. Casserley*

traffic in passenger livery, but Nos. 823-37 were goods black until 1930-5.

All were run-in by Eastleigh shed, usually on the Salisbury goods or Bournemouth slows, and then allocated to: Exmouth Junction Nos. 823-7; Salisbury Nos. 828-32; Feltham Nos. 833-7. They were well received by the men as the longer valve travel, improved draughting and post-Bridge Testing Committee balancing made them faster, free-running and more economical than the Urie 'S15s', with the result that greater use was made of them on the passenger services, especially west of Salisbury. However, for working heavy main line goods, some Feltham crews preferred the original series, particularly in bad weather.

In 1928 an extensive and often quite bewildering series of tender exchanges commenced on the Western and Eastern Sections involving this class, the 'King Arthurs' and 'Lord Nelsons'. Since these exchanges extended over nine years, the following code has been used to clarify the various types of tenders involved:

F/T: Urie pattern 5,000 gallon double bogie tender with a flared top, weighing 57 tons 11 cwt.
F/T/A: Similar to the F/T tender, but having auxiliary vacuum cylinders on the tank tops, weighing 57 tons 16 cwt.
F/S: The Maunsell development of the F/T/A tender with flush sides and partial welded construction, weighing 56 ton 8 cwt.
A/4: Ashford pattern 4,000 gallon six-wheel tender, weighing 42 tons 8 cwt.

The first exchanges concerned the transfer of F/S tenders from Nos. 833-7 to 'Lord Nelson' class Nos. 851/4-7 and their replacement by F/T tenders left spare

when Eastern Section 'King Arthurs' Nos. 763/4/8/71/2 received the small A/4 pattern. Details are:

| No. | F/T Tender from | Date | F/S Tender to |
|---|---|---|---|
| 833 | 764 | 5/1928 | 851 |
| 834 | 763 | 8/1928 | 854 |
| 835 | 768 | 9/1928 | 855 |
| 836 | 771 | 11/1928 | 856 |
| 837 | 772 | 11/1928 | 857 |

This exchange was brought about by the need to provide newly built 'Lord Nelsons' Nos. 851/4-7 with the most modern available tenders.

These exchanges had no sooner been completed when the F/T/A tenders of Nos. 828-32 were required to replace the small A/4 pattern on 'Lord Nelsons' Nos. 852/3 and to provide tenders for Nos. 858-60 under construction at Eastleigh Works. In their place Nos. 828-32 received the F/T tenders left spare when Eastern Section 'King Arthurs' Nos. 765-7/9/70 were allotted small A/4 tenders. Details are:

| No. | F/T Tender from | Date | F/T/A Tender to |
|---|---|---|---|
| 828 | 770 | 1/1929 | 858 |
| 829 | 766 | 2/1929 | 859 |
| 830 | 765 | 3/1929 | 860 |
| 831 | 769 (a) | 12/1929 | 852 |
| 832 | 767 | 2/1930 | 853 |

(a) During these exchanges No. 769 was transferred from Battersea to the Western Section and therefore did not require a small A/4 tender; instead it received a new F/S pattern.

'S15' No. 832 in goods black at Salisbury on 28th April 1928, as built with Urie pattern double bogie tender.          *H. C. Casserley*

'S15' No. 832 in Maunsell passenger livery and smoke deflectors at Eastleigh c.1934.          *Collection R. S. Carpenter*

'S15' No. 836 in Maunsell passenger livery with smoke deflectors and Ashford pattern 4,000 gallon six-wheeled tender c.1937. *O. J. Morris*

The final pre-war tender exchanges were a straight swap between 'S15s' Nos. 833-7, which required small A/4 tenders for service on the Central Section, and Eastern Section 'King Arthurs' Nos. 763-7, whose tenders of this pattern fitted in 1928-30 had caused problems when they were loaned by Nine Elms. Details are:

| No. | A/4 Tender from | Date | F/T Tender to |
|---|---|---|---|
| 833 | 763 | 10/1936 | 763 (a) |
| 834 | 764 | 11/1936 | 764 |
| 835 | 765 | 12/1936 | 765 |
| 836 | 766 | 7/1937 | 766 |
| 837 | 767 | 5/1937 | 767 |

(a) No. 833 lost its F/T tender to 'N15X' No. 2329 in November 1934 and ran with Drummond 4,000 gallon tender off 'C8' No. 294 until March 1935, when it received the F/T tender from Urie 'S15' No. 508. This was the tender transferred to No. 763 in October 1936.

At the end of these exchanges the tender position was:

| | |
|---|---|
| F/T (5,000 gallon, flared topped) | Nos. 823-32 |
| F/S (5,000 gallon, flush-sided) | Nos. 838-47 |
| A/4 (4,000 gallon, six-wheeled) | Nos. 833-7 |

On the Central Section Nos. 833-7 were stationed at Brighton and replaced 'K' class Nos. 2343/5/8/9/51 on the following goods turns:

Duty 695 (Tues, Thur, Sat): 2.10 a.m. Hove-Battersea Yard (arr. 5.15 a.m.)
(Weds, Fri): 12.01 a.m. Battersea Yard-Brighton (arr. 3.10 a.m.)
(Suns): 12.49 a.m. Battersea Yard-Brighton (arr. 4.25 a.m.)
Duty 697 (Daily): 3.00 a.m. Brighton-Three Bridges (arr. 6.22 a.m.)
(Weekdays): 9.35 a.m. Three Bridges-New Cross Gate (arr. 12.32 p.m.)
9.28 p.m. Bricklayers Arms-Brighton (arr. 12.18 a.m.)
(Sats only): 9.35 a.m. Three Bridges-Horley (arr. 9.45 a.m.)
light engine to Norwood Yard
2.38 p.m. Norwood-New Cross Gate (arr. 2.58 p.m.)
7.06 p.m. Bricklayers Arms-Norwood Yard
11.30 p.m. Norwood Yard-Hove (arr. 5.03 a.m.)
Duty 698 (Daily): 9.45 p.m. Brighton-Bricklayers Arms (arr. 12.05 a.m.)
2.30 a.m. New Cross Gate-Hove (arr. 4.55 a.m.)
Duty 699 (Daily): 11.45 p.m. Hove-East Croydon (arr. 1.49 a.m.)
light engine to Norwood Yard via Selhurst.
3.40 a.m. Norwood Yard-Hove (arr. 5.45 a.m.)
7.01 a.m. Hove-Holland Road (arr. 7.06 a.m.)

With only four booked duties, Nos. 833-7 were not over-worked, but nevertheless their immense power, good acceleration and strong braking were much appreciated on the busy Central Section main line. They were prohibited from working passenger and empty carriage stock trains or exceeding 45 mph, although without speedometers how drivers were expected to estimate their speed to such exactitude, especially after dark, is difficult to comprehend.

On the Western Section no such inhibitions existed and the class regularly appeared on the Salisbury-Exeter and Salisbury-Waterloo semi-fasts, while on summer Saturdays 'King Arthurs' and 'N15s' were deputised on the West of England, Bournemouth, ocean liner and Channel Island reliefs. Probably because of this extensive passenger usage the black goods livery was replaced by passenger green from December 1929. Around the same period smoke deflectors were fitted and the E-prefix discarded, these dates and those for the livery change are:

| No. | Smoke Deflectors | Passenger Livery | E-prefix Discarded |
|---|---|---|---|
| 823 | 2/1930 | 2/1930 | 4/1932 |
| 824 | 5/1931 | 5/1931 | 9/1932 |
| 825 | 3/1932 | 3/1932 | 3/1932 |
| 826 | 11/1931 | 11/1931 | 11/1931 |
| 827 | 1/1930 | 1/1930 | 1/1932 |
| 828 | 1/1930 | 1/1930 | 7/1931 |
| 829 | 5/1930 | 5/1935 (a) | 9/1931 |
| 830 | 4/1930 | 3/1935 (a) | 9/1932 |
| 831 | 12/1929 | 12/1929 | 10/1932 |
| 832 | 2/1930 | 2/1930 | 10/1932 |
| 833 | 7/1930 | 4/1933 | 10/1932 |
| 834 | 5/1930 | 3/1935 (a) | 11/1932 |
| 835 | 4/1930 | 5/1932 | 5/1932 |
| 836 | 7/1930 | 7/1930 | 3/1932 |
| 837 | 6/1930 | 6/1930 | 9/1932 |

(a) Nos. 829/30/4 received heavy repairs at Eastleigh Works in April and May 1930, but because of the stringent economy measures

'S15' No. 847 at Bedhampton on 6th June 1937, just six months after entering service, with the partially welded flush-sided Maunsell double bogie tender.

*H. E. Simmons*

'S 15' No. 844 in wartime black with Bulleid lettering and cabside numerals before the removal of snifting valves at the end of 1947.
*R. Randell Collection*

then in force, only had the black livery touched-up and revarnished. This also applied to the September-December 1932 intermediate repairs; consequently it was March-May 1935 before the green livery was received.

The 1936-7 Central Section transfers were replaced on the Western Section by newly constructed Nos. 843-7, while Nos. 838-42 of this series broke new ground by being sent to the Eastern Section. This gave a mid-1927 allocation of: Feltham Nos. 843-6; Salisbury Nos. 828-32; Exmouth Junction Nos. 823-7/47; Brighton Nos. 833-7; Hither Green Nos. 838-42.

At Hither Green Nos. 838-42 replaced 'N' class 2—6—0s Nos. 1868-70/3-5 on duties 180-3, their details being:

Duty 180 (Monday, Wednesday, Friday), Duty 181 (Tuesday, Thursday, Saturday): 1.20 a.m. Hither Green sidings-Ashford-Dover Priory, 9.35 p.m. Dover Town-Bricklayers Arms.
Duty 182 (Mondays-Saturdays): 5.50 a.m. Hither Green sidings-Ashford, 12.20 p.m. Ashford-Hither Green sidings.
Duty 183 (Mondays-Fridays): 4.20 a.m. Hither Green sidings-Dover Priory, 5.30 p.m. Dover Priory-Ashford-Hither Green sidings.

The spare engine was usually employed on transfer goods to Feltham. Like those stationed on the Central Section, all passenger work was prohibited and the speed restricted to 45 mph.

At Feltham Nos. 843-6 worked goods duties to Reading, Willesden, Eastleigh, Fratton, Southampton, Bournemouth and Dorchester, but Salisbury's Nos. 828-32, apart from one Southampton docks working, were restricted to the West of England line. Most of these duties covered Salisbury-Exmouth Junction goods, but on summer Saturdays there were two booked slow passenger turns to Exeter and the smartly timed 2.40 p.m. Sidmouth Junction-Salisbury (1.48 p.m. from Exmouth). Nos. 823-7/47 of Exmouth Junction were similarly restricted during the week, although their Salisbury goods duties were inter-

spersed by a number of slow passenger workings and the Templecombe-Salisbury milk tankers. In addition to the booked duties there were summer Saturday reliefs, ballast trains and van specials.

The Bulleid livery changes first affected the class in mid-1939, details being:

Maunsell green, black and yellow lining, tender numerals: Nos. 843 (June 1939), 844 (August 1939), 847 (July 1939).
Maunsell green, black and yellow lining, Bulleid lettering, cabside numerals: No. 849 (September 1939).
Maunsell green, unlined, Bulleid lettering, cabside numerals: Nos. 842 (December 1939), Nos. 824/40/1 (April 1940), 829/30/9 (May 1940), 838 (June 1940), 826 (August 1940).
Malachite green, unlined, Bulleid lettering, cabside numerals: Nos. 825/7 (October 1940), 831 (November 1940), 833 (January 1941), 836 (February 1941).

Later repaints, commencing with No. 823 in March 1941, were plain black with Bulleid lettering and cabside numerals, a drab livery which was brightened from September 1941 by the use of green shaded (sunshine) lettering and numerals. The first Eastleigh engine in this style was No. 845.

Nos. 838-42 were transferred to Feltham in October 1939 and replaced at Hither Green by 'King Arthurs' Nos. 765/8/9/94/6, 801/6, but otherwise the war had little effect on the class until the fall of France. At once, on Government instructions, all non-essential engines were evacuated from the coastal sheds to avoid possible destruction or capture by the Germans, so Nos. 833-7 were transferred to New Cross Gate and their Central Section goods duties adjusted for operation from the London end of the line. Nevertheless, No. 836 was shot up with 20 mm cannon shells on 12th October 1942, while standing outside Brighton Works. Damage was not serious and it was back in traffic by the end of the month.

'S15' No. 30837 in BR plain black livery, with Ashford 4,000 gallon six-wheeled tender and first totem, but after removal of the temporary S-prefix.
*R. H. Tunstall*

'S15' No. 30829, with Urie pattern 5,000 gallon double bogie tender, shortly after repainting in BR unlined black.
*Photomatic*

'S15' No. 30842 with flush-sided Maunsell double bogie tender and large BR totem at Salisbury on 8th May 1954. *W. Gilburt*

No other changes of note occurred before December 1942, when ten 'N15s' were loaned to the LNER and their loss to Eastleigh made good by the transfer of 'King Arthurs' from Feltham and 'N' class 2—6—0s from Exmouth Junction. To replace those transfers, Feltham received Nos. 833-7 from New Cross Gate, where their duties were taken over by 'K' class 2—6—0s Nos. 2337/40/50/3. The 4,000 gallon tenders did not endear them to Western Section crews and consideration was given to exchanging them for the 5,000 gallon pattern off five Eastern Section 'King Arthurs', but the difficulty of withdrawing ten 4—6—0s from traffic in wartime proved too great and Nos. 833-7 were left to cope as best they could with their small tenders.

During the war Eastleigh was unable to accept all the engines normally repaired there and assistance had to be sought from Ashford and Brighton, with the former giving general repairs and repaints to Nos. 830/1/46 in April-June 1942 and Brighton to No. 836 in February 1941. The last mentioned establishment in 1942-4 also repaired eleven 'N15' and seventeen 'King Arthur' boilers.

The allocation was unchanged after the 1942 transfers until November 1946, when Nos. 844-6 were transferred to Exmouth Junction, where they were followed by No. 843 in January 1948 and Nos. 841/2 in mid-year. This gave an allocation of: Feltham Nos. 833-40; Salisbury Nos. 828-32; Exmouth Junction Nos. 823-7/41-7.

All entered British Railways stock at Nationalisation to be be renumbered into the 30,000 series and painted goods black. Prior to this two carried the temporary S-prefix, details being:

S837 from 28/2/1948 to 24/4/1948
S838 from 29/2/1948 to 26/8/1949

The dates of renumbering and the removal of the smokebox snifting valves are:

| No. | BR No. | BR Livery | Snifting Valves Removed |
|---|---|---|---|
| 823 | 9/1948 | 9/1948 | 9/1948 |
| 824 | 1/1950 | 1/1950 | 1/1950 |
| 825 | 5/1948 | 5/1948 | 5/1948 |
| 826 | 5/1949 | 5/1949 | 5/1949 |
| 827 | 4/1949 | 4/1949 | 4/1949 |
| 828 | 12/1949 | 12/1949 | 8/1947 |
| 829 | 12/1948 | 12/1948 | 12/1948 |
| 830 | 3/1950 | 3/1950 | 12/1947 |
| 831 | 3/1949 | 9/1950 | 3/1949 |
| 832 | 9/1948 | 9/1948 | 9/1948 |
| 833 | 1/1949 | 8/1950 | 2/1948 |
| 834 | 2/1949 | 2/1949 | 11/1947 |
| 835 | 9/1948 | 9/1950 | 10/1949 |
| 836 | 9/1949 | 5/1950 | 10/1947 |
| 837 | 4/1948 | 2/1948 (a) | 2/1948 |
| 838 | 8/1949 | 2/1948 (a) | 2/1948 |
| 839 | 10/1948 | 12/1949 | 12/1949 |
| 840 | 8/1949 | 8/1949 | 3/1948 |
| 841 | 10/1948 | 10/1948 | 11/1947 |
| 842 | 9/1949 | 9/1949 | 3/1948 |
| 843 | 6/1948 | 8/1949 | 1/1948 |
| 844 | 7/1950 | 7/1950 | 12/1947 |
| 845 | 3/1948 | 3/1948 | 3/1948 |
| 846 | 4/1948 | 4/1948 | 4/1948 |
| 847 | 8/1948 | 8/1948 | 8/1948 |

(a) BR black with temporary S-prefix.

In January 1950 No. 30827 was transferred to Salisbury where it was followed by No. 30826 in August 1950 and Nos. 30823-5/47 in June 1951, while Nos. 30835-7

'S15' No. 30823 with an up freight at Seaton Junction on 24th July 1958.      *R. C. Riley*

replaced 'N' class 2–6–0s Nos. 31857/8/62 at Redhill on the Reading, Woking, Tonbridge and Ashford goods, ballast hopper specials and occasional Reading branch and Tonbridge stopping passenger trains. As a result of these transfers the allocation became: Salisbury Nos. 30823-32/47; Feltham Nos. 30833/4/8-40; Exmouth Junction Nos. 30841-6; Redhill Nos. 30835-7.

The Redhill duties were extended in June 1960 to include goods to Norwood and New Cross Gate, which led to the allocation being increased to four with the transfer of No. 30847 from Salisbury. Although no longer necessary, its 5,000 gallon tender (F/S) was replaced before transfer by the 3,500 gallon Ashford six-wheel pattern from withdrawn 'King Arthur' No. 30797 *Sir Blamor de Ganis*. No. 30807 was transferred to Feltham in June 1961, but Nos. 30835/6/47 remained working from Redhill until the goods services were dieselised in June 1963, when they were also despatched to Feltham.

Apart from No. 30847, three others also had their tenders exchanged at this period, details being:

| No. | Date | Tender from | Tender Type | Capacity gallons |
|---|---|---|---|---|
| 30833 | 5/1962 | 30908 | A/4 (a) | 4,000 |
| 30825 | 12/1963 | 30499 | F/T | 5,000 |
| 30837 | 6/1962 | 30912 | A/4 (a) | 4,000 |
| 30847 | 6/1960 | 30805 | A/3 (b) | 3,500 |

(a) Ashford pattern, six-wheeled with raves turned inwards for service with the 'School' class.
(b) Ashford pattern, six-wheeled built with Central Section 'King Arthurs' Nos. 793-806.

In the latter half of 1962 diesels reached Eastleigh and Feltham in force and as soon as crew training was completed they became available for main line goods service, consequently on 4th February 1963 the freight duties in the area bounded by London, Reading, Guildford, Fratton, Southampton, Dorchester and Salisbury were reorganised and mostly transferred to diesel operation. Prior to this and undoubtedly in anticipation, No. 30826 was condemned in November 1962. The West Country goods services remained steam-operated, but in December 1962 a readjustment of motive power responsibility saw Nos. 30841-6 of Exmouth Junction transferred to Western Region stock. No. 30846 was almost immediately withdrawn, with No. 30845 following in July 1963, but Nos. 30841-4 were replaced by 'N' class 2–6–0s Nos. 31812/21/54/9 in September 1963 and returned to the Southern Region. For several weeks Nos. 30842/4 were borrowed by Salisbury, but by late October 1963 all were working from Feltham.

Of the Feltham duties remaining steam-operated, two extended over three days, details being:

*Duties 104-6:*
Feltham-Reading and return, Waterloo-Eastleigh vans, Bevois Park sidings-Woking, Woking-Eastleigh-Chichester, stabled at Fratton, Portsmouth-Chichester vans, Chichester-Salisbury, Salisbury-Basingstoke, vans to Reading and return light engine, Morton Cutting sidings-Reading, Reading-Feltham and return, light engine to Basingstoke, Morton Cutting sidings-Reading, Reading-Earley and return, Reading-Feltham.

*Duties 112-4*
Clapham Junction-Southampton docks vans, light engine to Eastleigh for vans to Salisbury, returning with a goods, 5.00 p.m. South-

ampton Central-Bournemouth passenger, Poole-Eastleigh-Feltham, return trip to Nine Elms yard, Clapham Junction-Basingstoke vans, Basingstoke-Salisbury, Salisbury-Chichester, Chichester-Feltham.

There was one other booked turn, Duty 111, which covered two return goods to Reading, while special duties included empty coaching stock to and from Waterloo, ballast trains, substitutions for failed or damaged diesels and occasional secondary passenger trains. These duties kept the class fully occupied until 1964, when Nos. 30823/5/7/8/30/2/4-6/40/1/3/4/7 were withdrawn, leaving only Nos. 30824/33/7-9/42 in stock. Over the Christmas period Nos. 30824/39/42 were noted passing Basingstoke with West of England parcel trains, No. 30837 arriving at Southampton docks with a special goods, No. 30837 in charge of the 6.09 p.m. Waterloo-Basingstoke semi-fast and Nos. 30833/8/9 working London area goods and empty coaching stock. No. 30833 failed with faulty cylinders in May 1965, but the others remained active, with No. 30838 heading the through Bournemouth-York on 26th May 1965. All five survivors were condemned in September 1965, although at the beginning of the month No. 30838 spent several days working ECS and carriage piloting at Clapham Junction while No. 30839 was noted heading the 8.35 p.m. Salisbury-Basingstoke and a Reading-Oxford goods. After a period in store No. 30837 was steamed for working the S15 Commemorative Railtour from Waterloo to Eastleigh via

Alton on 9th January 1966. The return was over the Portsmouth Direct Line, renewing for the last time the S15's traditional relief passenger role. The tour was so heavily over-subscribed that it was repeated a week later. After these two outings No. 30837 returned to store until despatched at the end of the summer to Cashmores yard at Newport for breaking up.

## PRESERVATION

Nos. 30825/8/30/41/4/7 had the good fortune to be sold to Woodham Brothers, Barry, for to date only No. 30825 has been cannibalised and No. 30844 broken up. Of the others No. 30830 remains without a tender at Barry, while Nos. 30828/41/7 have been purchased for preservation. Details are:

No. 828 (boiler No. 781, tender No. 3227 from No. 830): Purchased for £10,500 by the Eastleigh Railway Preservation Society in November 1980 and transported to Eastleigh Works in March 1981 for refurbishment.

No. 841 (boiler No. 1409, tender No. 3238): Purchased for £4,000 by the Essex Locomotive Society Ltd. in July 1972 and moved to Chappel and Wakes Colne on the Stour Valley Railway in September 1972. The cost of transfer was sponsored by Greene, King & Sons Ltd., the East Anglian brewers, and in recognition it was named *Greene King*. Restoration proceeded rapidly and in Maunsell

'S15' No. 30824, in black livery with second BR totem, shunting an up pick-up goods at Whimple on 6th July 1961. *R. C. Riley*

'S15' No. 30843 arriving at Basingstoke with a freight from Woking on 25th July 1964.
*E. Wilmshurst*

green livery it was displayed at the late 1974 Stour Valley Railway open day. After taking part in the Cavalcade of Steam to commemorate the 150th anniversary of the opening of the Stockton & Darlington Railway, a number of railtours were worked and appearances in steam made on the Stour Valley Railway before being transferred to the Nene Valley Railway. Unfortunately, this line became committed to continental engines and rolling stock, so a further move was necessary if the expense and complication of fitting the Westinghouse air brake was to be avoided. This occurred in December 1978 to the North Yorkshire Moors Railway, where it was employed extensively in 1979-80 before being laid aside for heavy repairs, which commenced in early 1984.

No. 847 (boiler No. 456, tender No. 3225 from No. 828): Purchased for £10,350 by the Maunsell Locomotive Society in September 1978 and transported the following month to the Bluebell Railway.

## ENGINE SUMMARY

| No. | Date | Order No. | Mileage | Withdrawn |
|---|---|---|---|---|
| 823 | 3/1927 | E90 | 1,411,643 | 11/1964 |
| 824 | 3/1927 | " | 1,389,996 | 9/1965 |
| 825 | 4/1927 | " | 1,384,665 | 1/1964 |
| 826 | 5/1927 | " | 1,364,577 | 12/1962 |
| 827 | 6/1927 | " | 1,358,001 | 1/1964 |
| 828 | 7/1927 | " | 1,287,124 | 1/1964 |
| 829 | 7/1927 | " | 1,209,387 | 11/1963 |
| 830 | 8/1927 | " | 1,259,236 | 7/1964 |
| 831 | 9/1927 | " | 1,304,943 | 11/1963 |
| 832 | 10/1927 | " | 1,205,892 | 1/1964 |
| 833 | 11/1927 | E158 | 945,634 | 5/1965 |
| 834 | 11/1927 | " | 952,561 | 11/1964 |
| 835 | 12/1927 | " | 923,425 | 11/1964 |
| 836 | 12/1927 | " | 871,613 | 6/1964 |
| 837 | 1/1928 | " | 911,016 | 9/1965 |
| 838 | 5/1936 | E630 | 827,196 | 9/1965 |
| 839 | 5/1936 | " | 795,995 | 9/1965 |
| 840 | 6/1936 | " | 781,397 | 9/1964 |
| 841 | 7/1936 | " | 837,002 | 1/1964 |
| 842 | 8/1936 | " | 898,348 | 9/1968 |
| 843 | 9/1936 | " | 856,824 | 9/1964 |
| 844 | 10/1936 | " | 873,763 | 6/1964 |
| 845 | 10/1936 | " | 858,845 | 7/1963 |
| 846 | 11/1936 | " | 845,017 | 1/1963 |
| 847 | 12/1936 | " | 931,829 | 1/1964 |

All built by Eastleigh Works. Disposal: Broken up at Eastleigh Works Nos. 826/7/9/31/2/45/6. Sold: Woodham Brothers Nos. 825/8/30/41/4/7; J. Cashmore Nos. 823/4/36/7/42; J. Buttigieg No. 833; Birds Commercial Motors (Risca) Nos. 838/9; Birds Commercial Motors (Morriston) Nos. 834/5; Shipbreakers (Queenborough) Ltd. Nos. 840/3. Of those sold Nos. 828/41/7 were later reprieved for preservation.

# Summary of Urie Classes

## ENGINES DESIGNED BY ROBERT URIE

### 4–6–0s

| | | |
|---|---|---|
| 'H15' class (1914) | Nos. 335, 482-91 | 11 |
| 'N15' class (1918-23) | Nos. 736-55 | 20 |
| 'S15' class (1920-1) | Nos. 496-515 | 20 |
| | | 51 |

### 4–6–2 tanks

| | | |
|---|---|---|
| 'H16' class (1921-2) | Nos. 516-20 | 5 |

### 4–8–0 tanks

| | | |
|---|---|---|
| 'G16' class (1921) | Nos. 492-5 | 4 |
| | | 60 |

'N15s' Nos. 753-5 were completed after Grouping.

## URIE CLASSES MODIFIED AND BUILT BY R. E. L. MAUNSELL

### 4–6–0s

| | | |
|---|---|---|
| 'H15' class (1924-5) | Nos. 330-4, 473-8, 521-4 | 15 |
| 'King Arthur' class (1925-7) | Nos. 448-57, 763-806 | 54 |
| 'S15' class (1927-36) | Nos. 823-47 | 25 |
| | | 94 |

# L.S.W.R. Engine Stock

## NUMBER OF ENGINES STATIONED AT THE LOCOMOTIVE DEPOTS

| | March 1899 | December 1922 |
|---|---|---|
| Nine Elms | 190 | 162 |
| Strawberry Hill | 38 | 58 |
| Ascot | 1 | 2 |
| Windsor | 8 | 7 |
| Reading | 2 | 1 |
| Leatherhead | 2 | 4 |
| Hampton Court | 4 | — |
| Chertsey | 2 | 1 |
| Woking | — | 4 |
| Guildford | 50 | 69 |
| Ash | — | 1 |
| Basingstoke | 6 | 14 |
| Northam/Eastleigh | 81 (12 at Soton Dks) | 108 |
| Gosport | 1 | 1 |
| Bishops Waltham | 1 | — |
| Fratton | 22 | 33 |
| Midhurst | 1 | — |
| Southampton Docks | 12 | 14 |
| Lymington | 1 | 1 |
| Bournemouth | 18 | 36 |
| Ringwood | 1 | 1 |
| Hamworthy Junction | 3 | 4 |
| Wimborne | 2 | 4 |
| Swanage | 1 | 1 |
| Dorchester | 11 | 14 |
| Weymouth | 4 | 4 |
| Andover Junction | 4 | 3 |
| Salisbury | 36 | 61 |
| Templecombe | 1 | 1 |
| Yeovil | 17 | 16 |
| Chard | 1 | Closed |
| Seaton | 1 | 1 |
| Lyme Regis | Not opened | 1 |
| Sidmouth | 1 | 1 |
| Budleigh Salterton | 1 | Closed |
| Exmouth | 1 | 5 |
| Exmouth Junction | 60 | 81 (1 at Sidmouth) |
| Barnstaple | 7 | 11 (2 at Torrington) |
| Ilfracombe | 1 | 3 |
| Torrington | 3 | 2 |
| Okehampton | 1 | 2 (1 at Bude) |
| Holsworthy | 1 | Closed |
| Bude | 1 | 1 |
| Launceston | 1 | 1 |
| Wadebridge | 7 | 7 (1 at Launceston) |
| Devonport | 2 | Closed |
| Plymouth Friary | 9 | 17 |
| Total at Depots | 618 | 758 |
| In or awaiting works | 69 | 83 |
| Stored unserviceable | 20 | 47 |
| Stored serviceable | — | 24 |
| Total engine stock | 707 | 912 |

URIE 'H15' MIXED TRAFFIC 4-6-0

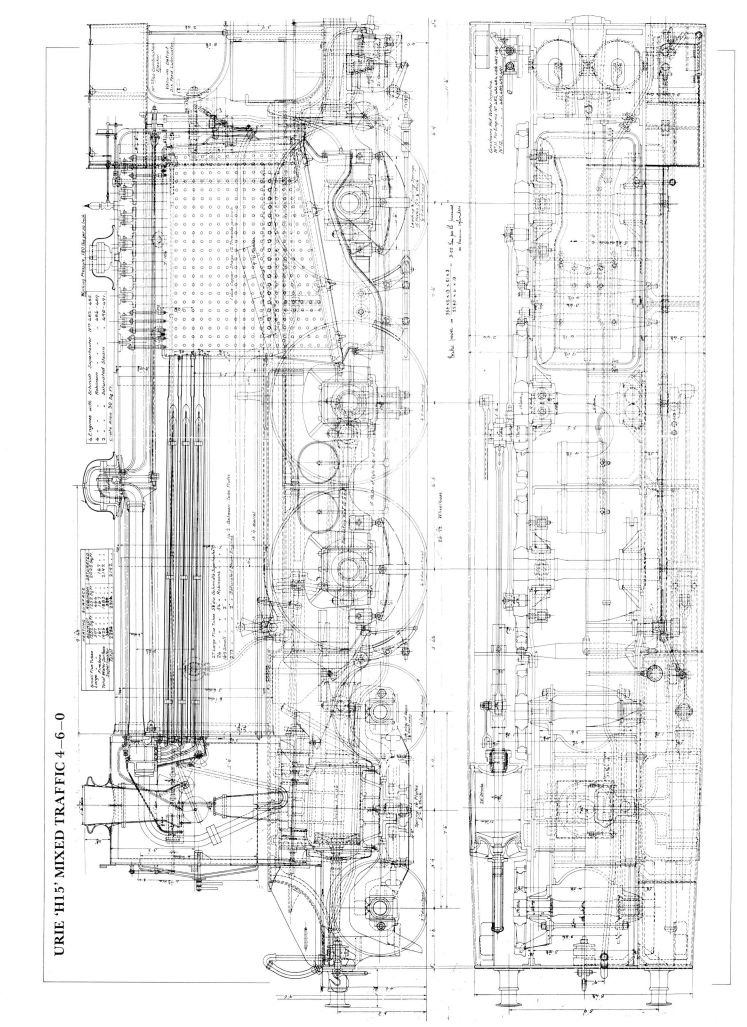

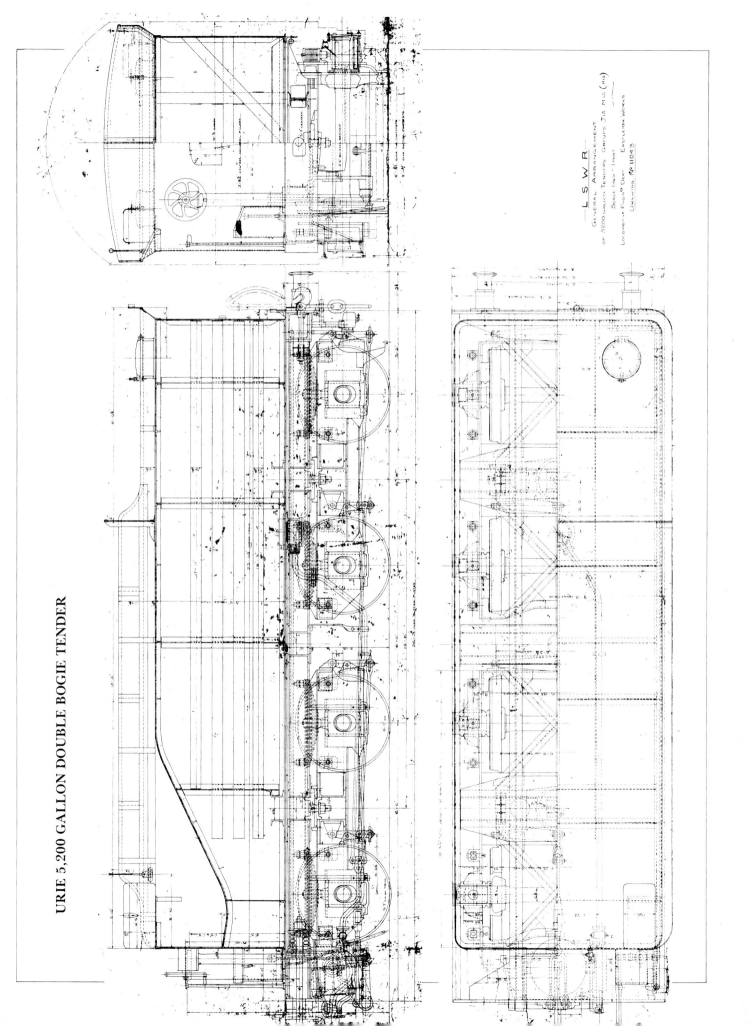

URIE 5,200 GALLON DOUBLE BOGIE TENDER

L S W R
General Arrangement
of 5200 Gallon Tenders (Groups J.15 M.5 (H5))
Scale Half Inch = 1 Foot
Locomotive Engr's Dept    Eastleigh Works
Drawing No 11043

'N15' EXPRESS 4–6–0

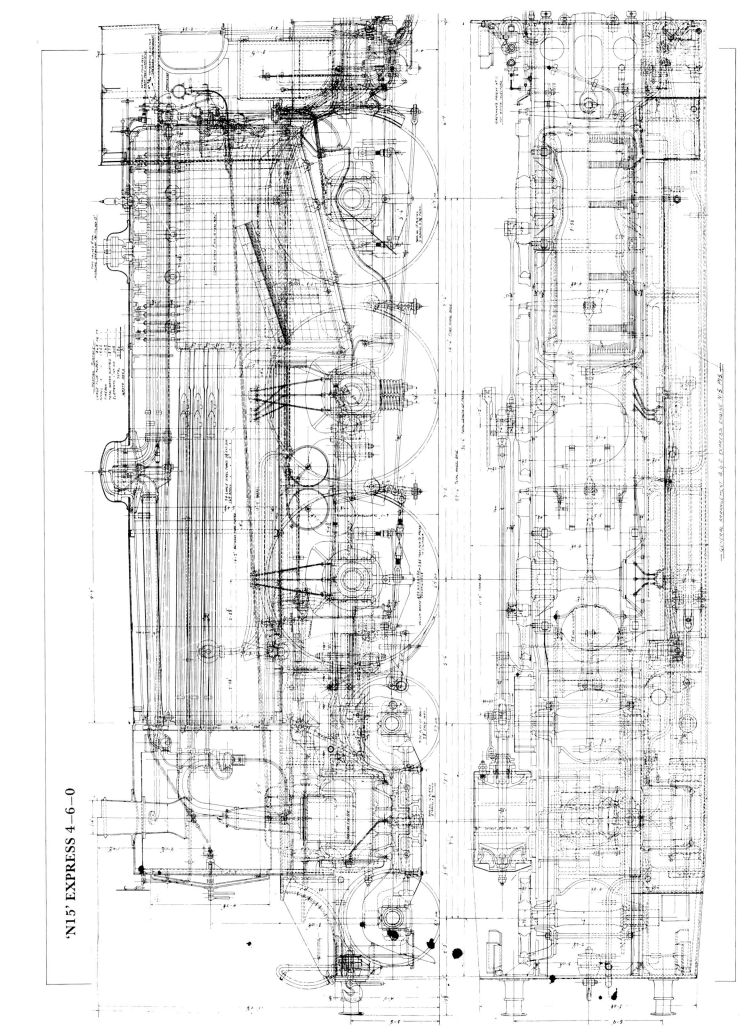

GENERAL ARRANGEMENT 4 6 0 EXPRESS ENGINE N15 PLS

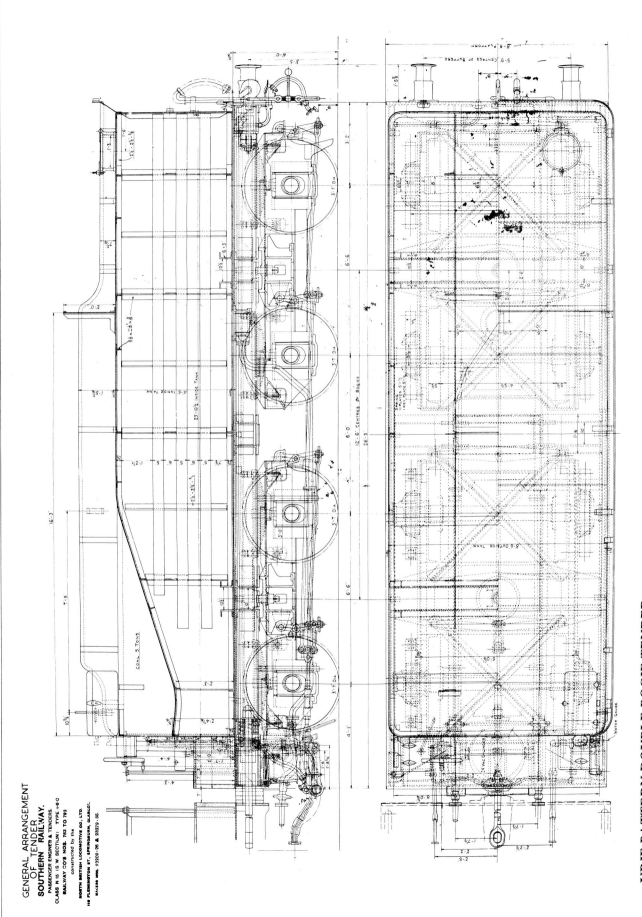

GENERAL ARRANGEMENT
OF TENDER
SOUTHERN RAILWAY.
PASSENGER ENGINES & TENDERS.
CLASS N 15 (S. W. SECTION) TYPE 4-6-0
RAILWAY CO'S NOS. 783 TO 792
constructed by the
NORTH BRITISH LOCOMOTIVE CO. LTD.
110 FLEMINGTON ST., SPRINGBURN, GLASGOW.
MAKERS NOS. 23209-26 & 23279-92.

URIE PATTERN DOUBLE BOGIE TENDER
constructed by North British Locomotive Co. Ltd.

'S15' GOODS 4-6-0

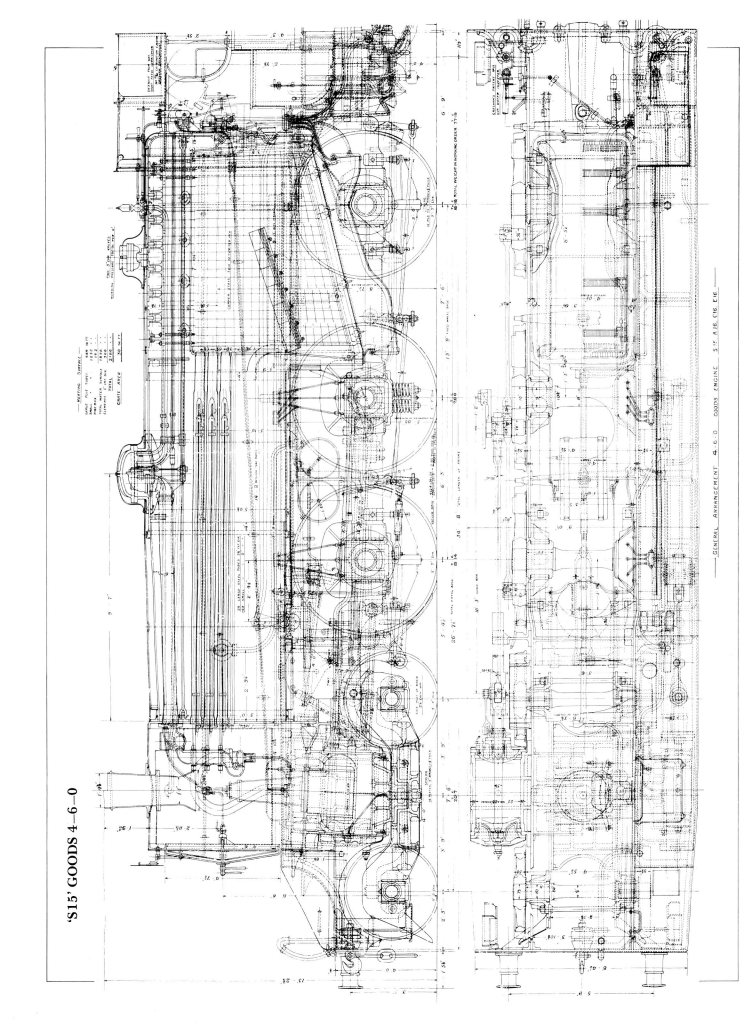

GENERAL ARRANGEMENT 4-6-0 GOODS ENGINE S15 A16, C16, E16

# URIE 5,000 GALLON DOUBLE BOGIE TENDER
## with feed water heater

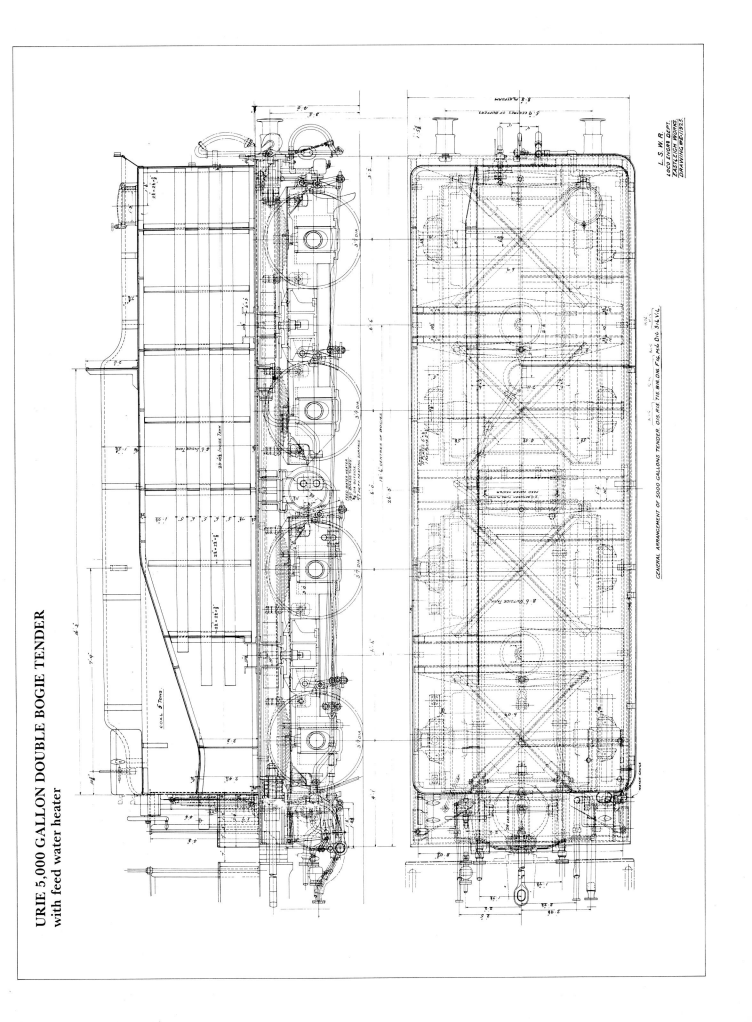

GENERAL ARRANGEMENT OF 5000 GALLONS TENDER. O15 R15 T15 B16 D16 F16 M16 D16 S16 V16.

L. S. W. R.
LOCO ENGRS DEPT.
EASTLEIGH WORKS
DRAWING ME1/1923.

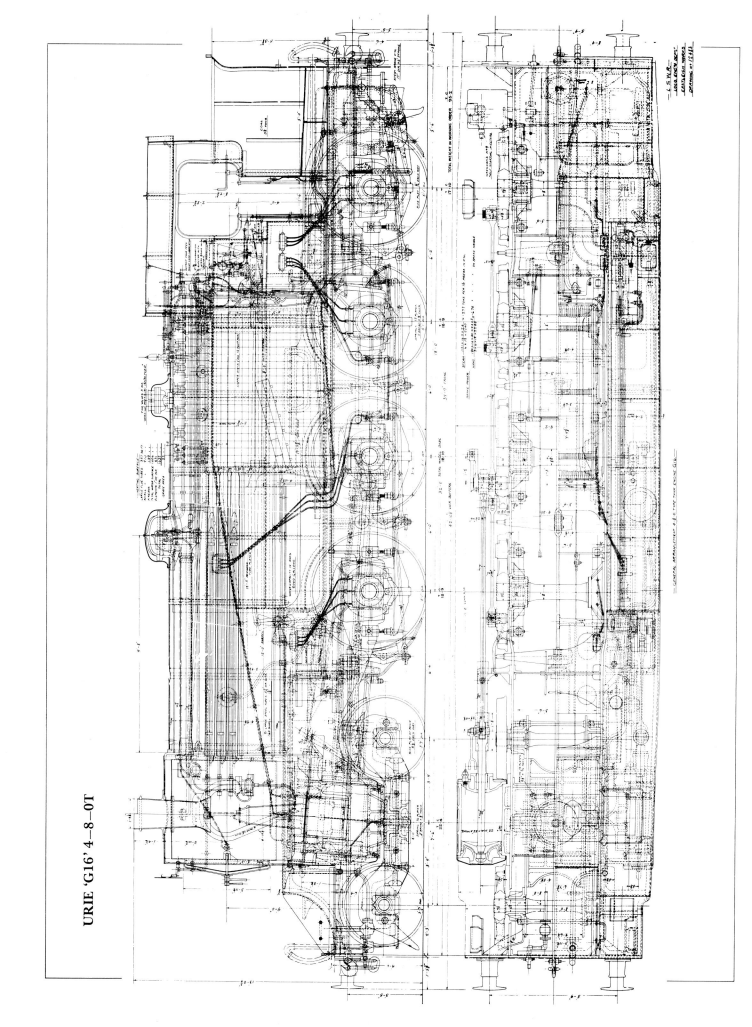

URIE 'G16' 4–8–0T

L.S.W.R.
LOCO ENGRS DEPT
EASTLEIGH WORKS
DRAWING № 12413

GENERAL ARRANGEMENT 4-8-0 TYPE TANK ENGINE G16

**URIE 'H16' 4–6–2T**

L.S.W.R.
LOCO. and C.M.E.
EASTLEIGH WORKS
DRAWING N° 12337

— GENERAL ARRANGEMENT OF 4.6.2. TYPE. TANK ENGINE H16. —

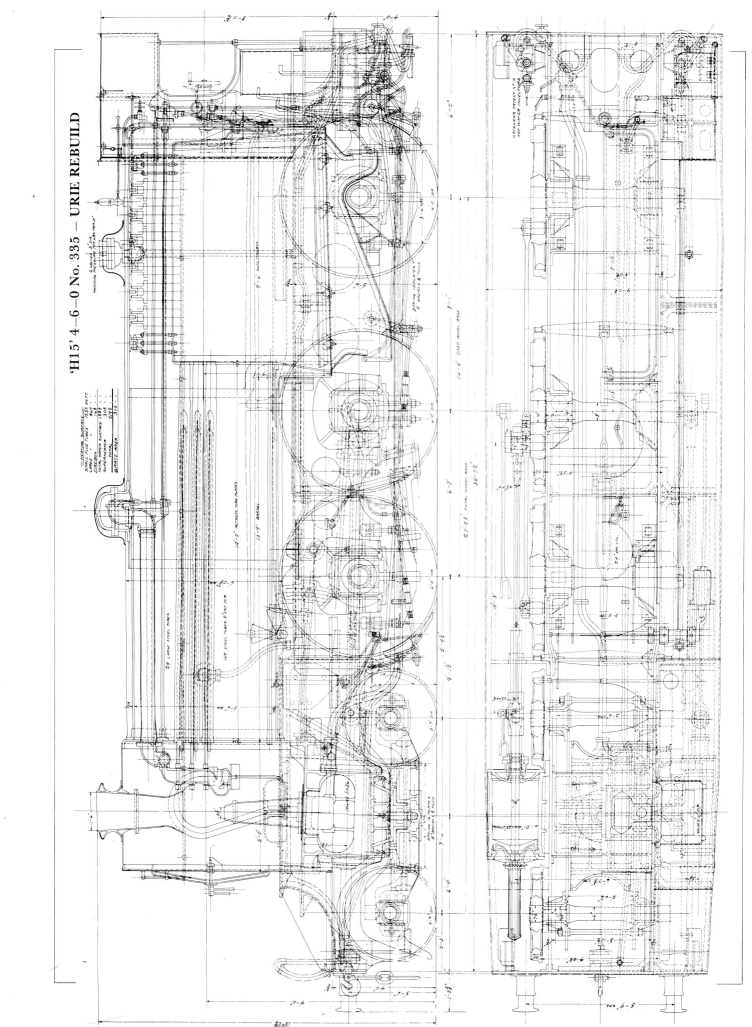

'H15' 4–6–0 No. 335 – URIE REBUILD